Thomas C. Rowe, PhD

Federal Narcotics Laws and the War on Drugs
Money Down a Rat Hole

D0143763

Pre-publication
REVIEWS,
COMMENTARIES,
EVALUATIONS . . .

"Thomas C. Rowe gives an informative, comprehensive, and critical review on the history of drug law legislation and convincingly argues how the current 'War on Drugs' continually fails because it is a misguided war on America's citizens. What becomes abundantly clear in this read is the strength of Rowe's thesis that the war is nothing more than blindly pouring large amounts of money down a never-ending rat hole. This author provides substantiated reasoning supporting the futility of interdiction and the repeated failure of incarcerating drug users and/or abusers. Rowe's emphasis on changing drug use through comprehensive drug education programs, drug treatment, the author's insights into the legalization debate, and his final recommendations for restructuring the control of drug use is not only well argued but also worthy of serious consideration. In summary, Rowe has written a well-organized, interesting, informative, and appealing book."

Peter J. Venturelli, PhD
Chair and Associate Professor
of Sociology and Criminology,
Valparaiso University

More pre-publication
REVIEWS, COMMENTARIES, EVALUATIONS . . .

"Compelling and original, this is the book I would have written for use in teaching my War on Drugs course. This book is an attempt to come up with a rational strategy to address the problems created by our attempts to solve other problems. It delves into the neglected history of education and treatment, and throughout references critical criminal justice concepts without being loaded with academic jargon or getting sidetracked on legalization debates. The federal government is taken to task for a fixation on marijuana, an inability to understand the criminal mind-set, especially when related to similarities and differences with the law-abiding mind-set, scare tactics and propaganda campaigns, and a failure to tell when policy goals are unreasonable. Overall, this book is a practical guide to restructuring priorities which takes a serious look at what a non-drug-free America might look like."

Tom O'Connor, PhD
Associate Professor of Justice Studies
and Applied Criminology,
North Carolina Wesleyan College;
Webmaster, MegaLinks in Criminal Justice

The Haworth Press
New York • London • Oxford

Federal Narcotics Laws and the War on Drugs
Money Down a Rat Hole

HAWORTH Addictions Treatment
F. Bruce Carruth, PhD
Senior Editor

Neuro-Linguistic Programming in Alcoholism Treatment edited by Chelly M. Sterman

Cocaine Solutions: Help for Cocaine Abusers and Their Families by Jennifer Rice-Licare and Katherine Delaney-McLoughlin

Preschoolers and Substance Abuse: Strategies for Prevention and Intervention by Pedro J. Lecca and Thomas D. Watts

Chemical Dependency and Antisocial Personality Disorder: Psychotherapy and Assessment Strategies by Gary G. Forrest

Substance Abuse and Physical Disability edited by Allen W. Heinemann

Addiction in Human Development: Developmental Perspectives on Addiction and Recovery by Jacqueline Wallen

Addictions Treatment for Older Adults: Evaluation of an Innovative Client-Centered Approach by Kathryn Graham, Sarah J. Saunders, Margaret C. Flower, Carol Birchmore Timney, Marilyn White-Campbell, and Anne Zeidman Pietropaolo

Group Psychotherapy with Addicted Populations: An Integration of Twelve-Step and Psychodynamic Theory, Second Edition by Philip J. Flores

Addiction Intervention: Strategies to Motivate Treatment-Seeking Behavior edited by Robert K. White and Deborah George Wright

Assessment and Treatment of the DWI Offender by Alan A. Cavaiola and Charles Wuth

Countertransference in Chemical Dependency Counseling by Gary G. Forrest

Solutions for the "Treatment Resistant" Addicted Client: Therapeutic Techniques for Engaging Challenging Clients by Nicholas A. Roes

Shame, Guilt, and Alcoholism: Treatment Issues in Clinical Practice, Second Edition by Ronald T. Potter-Effron

Treating Co-Occurring Disorders: A Handbook for Mental Health and Substance Abuse Professionals by Edward L. Hendrickson, Marilyn Strauss Schmal, and Sharon C. Ekleberry

Designing, Implementing, and Managing Treatment Services for Individuals with Co-Occurring Mental Health and Substance Use Disorders: Blueprints for Action by Edward L. Hendrickson

Federal Narcotics Laws and the War on Drugs: Money Down a Rat Hole by Thomas C. Rowe

Managing Your Recovery from Addiction: A Guide for Executives, Senior Managers, and Other Professionals by David F. O'Connell and Deborah Bevvino

Federal Narcotics Laws
and the War on Drugs
Money Down a Rat Hole

Thomas C. Rowe, PhD

The Haworth Press
New York • London • Oxford

For more information on this book or to order, visit
http://www.haworthpress.com/store/product.asp?sku=5536

or call 1-800-HAWORTH (800-429-6784) in the United States and Canada
or (607) 722-5857 outside the United States and Canada

or contact orders@HaworthPress.com

The Haworth Press, Inc., 10 Alice Street, Binghamton, NY 13904-1580.

PUBLISHER'S NOTE
The development, preparation, and publication of this work has been undertaken with great care. However, the Publisher, employees, editors, and agents of The Haworth Press are not responsible for any errors contained herein or for consequences that may ensue from use of materials or information contained in this work. The Haworth Press is committed to the dissemination of ideas and information according to the highest standards of intellectual freedom and the free exchange of ideas. Statements made and opinions expressed in this publication do not necessarily reflect the views of the Publisher, Directors, management, or staff of The Haworth Press, Inc., or an endorsement by them.

Cover design by Kerry E. Mack.

Library of Congress Cataloging-in-Publication Data

Rowe, Thomas C.
    Federal narcotics laws and the war on drugs : money down a rat hole / Thomas C. Rowe.
       p. cm.
    Includes bibliographical references and index.
    ISBN-13: 978-0-7890-2807-5 (hard : alk. paper)
    ISBN-10: 0-7890-2807-7 (hard : alk. paper)
    ISBN-13: 978-0-7890-2808-2 (soft : alk. paper)
    ISBN-10: 0-7890-2808-5 (soft : alk. paper)
    1. Drugs of abuse—Law and legislation—United States. 2. Drugs of abuse—United States—History. I. Title.

KF3890.R69 2006
344.7304'46—dc22
                                                                    2005023016

CONTENTS

ABOUT THE AUTHOR

Thomas C. Rowe, PhD, is Professor of Psychology at the University of Wisconsin–Stevens Point, where he has taught a course in psychoactive drugs for nearly thirty years. He wrote the Instructor's Manual for *Drugs and Human Behavior,* Second Edition.

Preface

I have been teaching a course in recreational drug usage at the University of Wisconsin-Stevens Point for nearly thirty years. The course was originally developed because our entering students were often very naive about alcohol and other drugs. This was a concern because alcohol abuse is common among college students and many of them would be exposed to illegal drugs for the first time. I felt that if they knew the whole truth about drugs of abuse they would be better able to make good decisions for themselves. I still believe that is true today, and that it could also be applied to a large segment of the U.S. population. However, my intent here is slightly different. This book does not focus on drugs per se; it focuses on drug policies. We in the United States need a more rational drug policy if we are ever going to have much impact on drug abuse in this country.

The current drug laws and policies were conceived largely in ignorance. Many were not even directed at drug problems, but rather were aimed at racial or ethnic groups. Since then, common myths and misconceptions about both drugs and U.S. drug policies have produced a situation in which we waste outrageous sums of money in ways that won't help us while starving the very programs that might actually benefit us.

The U.S. government and its agencies, in trying to fight a "War on Drugs," waste money and resources in three basic ways. First, we are spending most of our efforts and money attempting to interdict drugs. This includes trying to eliminate drug fields in the United States and abroad, trying to arrest smugglers, and trying to arrest the pushers and dealers who sell on the streets. Who could argue with such a policy? Every now and then a big drug bust makes the headlines, and this makes us all feel good; we think we are making a dent in the drug trade. Unfortunately, these efforts accomplish surprisingly little. In fact, we manage to stop only from about 10 to 30 percent of the drug

---

I would like to thank government documents librarian Marg Whalen for her help in digging out information.

flow (United Nations, 2000). Although this may have some positive impact, it should be obvious that interdiction at this level is never going to solve the problem. It doesn't matter how much more money or effort we spend this way; we are never going to solve the problem through interdiction efforts.

Second, when we actually catch offenders and arrest them, we put them in prison, thinking the punishment we give them will deter them from offending again as well as deter others from engaging in the same illegal activity. Unfortunately, past has shown that that didn't seem to have much of a deterrent effect, so we started imposing harsher and harsher penalties. This is a solution that was tried in the past, and it is being tried again in the present. It's a popular notion. We feel good about those penalties because we are punishing an evildoer. However, do harsh or even draconian penalties really work? The answer, perhaps surprisingly, is no. Harsh penalties and long prison terms serve only to expand an already burgeoning prison population at high cost to the public without actually deterring the crimes in question.

Third, when dealing with the entire range of illegal drugs, we spend a majority of our efforts going after the most benign and least damaging of them all: marijuana. This grows out of the mistaken belief that marijuana is a "gateway" drug to more harmful, more addictive drugs. We think that all we have to do is keep the gate closed and we will protect our youths from using even worse drugs. This is just a myth. No credible evidence exists that states marijuana is a gateway drug, or that eliminating it will keep people from trying other drugs. The result of this focus on marijuana is that money that could be spent more productively is funneled into this one area without having much effect on harm reduction.

In the process of doing the research to write this book, I made some surprising discoveries of my own. Among them is that it seems we are making some good decisions and some good trends are developing, especially during the past decade. We are spending more money than we used to on treatment, and educational efforts are growing. At the outset, I did not recognize how effective treatment programs have become or how much support they are receiving. We have come a long way in our ability to deal with addiction and abuse. I was also surprised to learn that education efforts were not as effective as I had assumed them to be. No matter how much or little effectiveness these two aspects of our response to illicit drugs have, spending our money and efforts on them is surely a better idea than continuing to throw the money away on policies that haven't worked in the past and will probably never work. Better ways of dealing with illicit drugs exist, and that is the point of this book.

Introduction

The United States is almost unique in the world today in terms of the magnitude of the country's drug abuse problems. This is partly reflected in our burgeoning prison populations and overcrowded courts. We incarcerate more people per capita than any other industrialized nation and the prime reason behind this is our so-called "War on Drugs" (see Chapter 5). Many people agree that we are either losing or have already lost that war. Very few people suggest we are winning or have any realistic hope of winning it. The reasons for this are varied, but mostly it seems to be because we consistently confuse a moral stance ("let's get tough on drugs") with measures of effectiveness. Any action that supports a moral position, such as harsh prison sentences for using or selling an illicit drug, is seen as effective while any other possibility is rejected. The result is a social policy that leads us to pour money down a rat hole with no end in sight. This book attempts to examine that rat hole in the light of reason.

It is important to recognize at the outset what this book is not. It is not an attempt to make the case that some currently illegal drugs should be made legal or decriminalized. Indeed, it is obvious that the great majority of recreational drugs are damaging and deserving of some form of regulatory control. Nor is this book a universal indictment of the federal government and its efforts to address the problem. Some of the current trends, such as financing state drug courts, subsidizing educational initiatives, and providing treatment for addicts in prison, are very positive. Unfortunately, some of the other actions of the government are distinctly harmful. The drug laws in the United States—even some of the modern revisions—were conceived largely in ignorance and often bear little or no relation to the drugs themselves, either in terms of damage to the individual user or in terms of damage to society. As a society we have lumped together substances that range from the benign to the deadly, and we attempt to impose sentences and spend resources on interdiction for the full range of that spectrum without regard to logic or even consequences. We have produced a social policy based on a unitary approach to banned substances without regard to distinctions between substances or whether that social policy does more harm than good. Not surprisingly, then, in numerous instances that social policy is damaging.

One contention of this book is that our current approach to recreational drugs is not a reasonable one. To be reasonable it would need to be applied equally across all addictive or recreational drugs, and of course it isn't; some recreational drugs are legal. One particular substance causes massive levels of ill health of all kinds and hundreds of thousands of premature deaths annually, yet is legal in any quantity for any adult. The only restrictions on it involve where it may be used and what age one must be to use it. Likewise, another substance that is legal for all adults is widely recognized as the number-one drug problem around the world. When sufficiently abused, it causes death by destroying the body, and even when not heavily abused, it causes aberrant behavior that can ruin families and damage society at large. Penalties for abusing this substance publicly and restrictions on how much may be used exist, but no law restricts how much may be possessed or how much may be used in privacy. Can there be anyone reading this who does not immediately recognize these two drugs? Yet tobacco and alcohol are legal while other drugs—which are different, to be sure, but are clearly no worse in their effects—remain completely criminalized. A rational drug policy that allows such discrepancies is difficult to envision. Unfortunately, it seems reasonably clear that any future drug policy will continue to have such inconsistencies built in. Judge Robert W. Sweet of the U.S. District Court of New York put it quite succinctly in a speech he made to Harvard Law School in May 1992:

> A public policy which permits the use and advertisement of alcohol and tobacco (which kill 400,000 annually), and a government policy which subsidizes tobacco, the most addictive of all drugs, cannot be reconciled with a mandatory 20 year prison term for a citizen who distributes a different form of mind-altering substance. (http://www.vcl.org/Judges/Sweet_J.htm)

Ignoring tobacco and alcohol for the moment, a unitary enforcement approach might be considered a reasonable social policy for illicit drugs if it had any realistic hope of success. However, it does not. Despite spending many resources on eliminating illicit drugs, very little evidence that we have any chance of winning the "War on

Drugs" exists. The record is long and dismal—failure. But it doesn't have to be that way. Some alternative strategies have a much greater chance of success than the current ones. This book includes a story of how the current system originated, an analysis of what's wrong with present approaches, and suggestions for changes.

In order to limit the scope, this work will concentrate on federal narcotic legislation and the effects of those laws. Even with this restriction the sheer volume of drug regulations passed by U.S. Congress from 1909 to the present makes a full review of them prohibitive. A U.S. House of Representatives report published in 1981 lists seventy-seven separate public laws passed by Congress between 1909 and 1980 on narcotics alone (Walsh, 1981). Each of those acts required committee hearings. For example, hearings that were not even associated with a specific bill were held on illicit narcotics traffic for the 84th Congress on June 2, 3, and 8, 1955, in the Judiciary Committee of the Senate. Those hearings generated a report 1,301 pages in length. Any comprehensive review of the totality of this material would by itself be extremely long.

Furthermore, we face a contradiction in terms. A dictionary definition of narcotic is "Any drug that induces profound sleep, lethargy, and relief of pain: it is usually an opiate." The tertiary definition is "Anything that causes drowsiness, lethargy, etc." Yet federal regulations classify opiates (including natural ones such as morphine, semisynthetics such as heroin, and synthetics such as fentanyls) and cocaine as narcotics. Originally, marijuana also was included in this category. Cocaine is a powerful stimulant; it could hardly be described as meeting the dictionary definition. Marijuana in large amounts might meet the definition, but it takes some effort to stretch it that far. Hence, by definition, the government classified together drugs that are radically different from each other in both effects and dangers. Medically or biologically speaking, only the opiate group should be classified as narcotics. Fortunately, the government stopped labeling marijuana a narcotic with the passage of the Comprehensive Drug Abuse Prevention and Control Act of 1970, but cocaine is still listed as a narcotic substance.

It may not be possible to effect much change in federal drug policy due to both political pressure and general ignorance. These factors can be addressed, but just as it is not possible to remake history, it may no longer be possible to reverse the unwanted effects of poorly

conceived legislation. To really understand the quagmire we find ourselves in, it will be necessary to examine the history of drug regulations, the problems the various acts and regulations were trying to address, and the basic outcomes of those efforts. This sounds like a
rather straightforward task, but things rarely prove to be as simple as
they appear. To at least some extent, the history of this legislation is
also a story of personalities. Three people in particular had major
impacts on the early development of drug policies. They were Hamilton Wright, William Randolph Hearst, and, most notably, Harry
J. Anslinger. All were driven by personal agendas and any truth or
evidence that conflicted with those agendas was discarded.

The first step along the path toward developing a more rational policy that will operate to effectively reduce damaging recreational drug
use is to understand how this situation began and to then examine to
what degree our current drug policies accomplish what we want them
to accomplish. In the process of doing this it will be necessary to
briefly discuss the nature of the drugs themselves. Furthermore, although there may be reasonable arguments why one drug or another
should or should not be legal, that is largely beyond the scope of this
book. (The basics of that debate are covered in Chapter 8.)

One specific suggestion that *will* be supported in this book is that
we should reapportion monies currently allocated to fight the "War
on Drugs" out of our current wasteful efforts at interdiction and into
prevention and treatment programs. Interdiction involves eliminating
the flow of illicit drugs, from the growing fields of the crops or the
laboratories at which they are made to the user/purchaser on the
street. We have not done a very good job at this and, in my opinion,
we have no reason to think we ever will. Prevention, largely dependent on education, should be used to convince people not to experiment with dangerous drugs. Every potential addict who chooses not
to start lessens the burden on society; this is surely the most efficient
use of public monies. This approach also minimizes drug-induced
damage. Providing adequately funded treatment for those who are already using drugs would also be far more productive in terms of reducing the impact of illicit drug abuse than would massive attempts at
interdiction. After all, when fewer people use a given substance, the
trafficking of that substance will decline naturally without any particular effort on the part of the public or law enforcement. In other
words, attacking the demand side of the equation is likely to solve the

interdiction problem, while continuing to spend heavily on interdiction is just wasting money.

This book will examine the laws themselves, how they came into being, and the consequences of their implementation. The current state of affairs in our "War on Drugs" will be discussed, and recommendations for policy change will be made.

Chapter 1

Narcotics and Narcotic Regulations to 1937

THE HISTORY OF OPIATES

Opium and the opiates—natural, semisynthetic, and fully synthetic—compose a class of drugs that are perhaps the most-often misunderstood by the general public. Opium itself is the dried sap from the seed pod of the *Papaver somniferum* plant. This substance has been known for 6,000 years or more and has been widely used in medicine and as a recreational substance since the time of the ancient Greeks (see Faupel, Horowitz, and Weaver, 2004, Chapter 2, for a history). In terms of medicine, no class of drug has been more useful than the opiates. The natural opiates include opium itself and tinctures of opium (such as paregoric or laudenum), morphine, and codeine. Other opiates include heroin, a semisynthetic opiate made by adding two acetyl groups to morphine, and fully synthetic opiates, which make up a very long list indeed. They include hydrocodone, propoxyphene, methadone, and the fentanyls.

Opiates have several properties that make them invaluable in medicine. Substitutes exist for these but, realistically, nothing works better or is less damaging than the opiates. Opiates have three characteristics that make them important to the medical field. First, they are analgesics. They are wonderful pain killers, and tend to operate on dull pain better than on sharp pains. They work to reduce the sensory input of pain in the brain, and also operate on the emotional response to pain, making it easier to tolerate. A second property is that they are antitussive, meaning they reduce coughing. Third, they operate directly on the intestinal wall to reduce peristaltic activity (rhythmic muscle contractions), making them great treatments for diarrhea.

Unfortunately, the opiates are also addictive drugs. They induce a physiological response to their use, which eventually produces a physical dependence and, because they also dull the mind to difficult situations in life, a psychological craving. The craving for their use is the real problem. Addicts have a very difficult time not returning to opiates even after they have succeeded in overcoming a physical dependence because they experience intense psychological cravings for the drug effects. The same mechanism in the brain (activation of the mu receptor) that dulls pain produces these cravings.

Physically, the opiates are really quite safe. Unlike alcohol, for instance, opiates do not damage the body even if a person is on high doses for extended periods of time. They also do not do any damage to the brain. It is possible to take a lethal dose, but (contrary to what we might be led to believe from television shows or movies), for an addict it takes a massive dose to be lethal (Brecher, 1972). The death that ensues is gradual and is caused by respiratory depression. Many people believe that narcotics, such as heroin, will cause degeneration of the mind or mental faculties. This is simply not true. In contrast to alcohol, which will damage the brain and cause mental deterioration when abused for long periods of time, heroin and the other narcotics are among the most benign of drugs. However, for those who are addicted, cravings will influence lifestyle choices in potentially unhealthy ways.

In order to understand why the United States eventually passed federal regulations to restrict the opiates, it is helpful to look at their use in the nineteenth and early twentieth centuries in the United States and in Europe. China also plays a major role.

Most opium in the nineteenth century was grown in India (which included modern Pakistan), Persia (Iran), and Afghanistan. The largest market for the processed opium was China. As early as 1729, China tried to ban opium (Hanson and Venturelli, 2001, p. 229) and at one time opium exports to China made up 14 percent of the official revenue of British India (Palfai and Jankiewicz, 1997, p. 371). Great Britain had a strong economic motivation to want the trade to China to proceed unimpeded. By 1839, China had realized opium addiction was a serious problem. The emperor Tao Kuang ordered strict enforcement of the regulation against importing opium. This caused a war with Great Britain. One result of this war, which ended in 1842, was the cession of Hong Kong to British control. Peace, of course, didn't last. The Second Opium War began in 1856 and ended in 1860 and was fought over Western demands that opium markets be expanded. The Chinese were again defeated. In 1858, by the Treaty of Tientsin, opium importation to China was formally legalized. Godfearing British traders claimed that the hardworking Chinese were entitled to "a harmless luxury"; the opium trade in less respectable hands would be taken over by "desperadoes, pirates and marauders" (BLTC Research, 2005). Soon, opium poured into China in unprecedented quantities. It has been estimated that, by the end of the nineteenth century, more than a quarter of the adult male Chinese population was addicted. Although the opium itself may not have been very damaging, the widespread use of it in opium dens posed the same kind of problems for China as would widespread alcoholism for the modern world. Imagine the effects on the economy alone if one-quarter of your country's workforce were alcoholic.

In the beginning of the twentieth century, the Boxer Rebellion in China began. Ostensibly, this was a movement to throw foreign influence out of China. Of course, the United States and Britain wanted China to be open to all foreign trade. Troops were once again sent to China and, once again, the Chinese were unable to compete with modern armed forces. The opium trade was saved for a third time. This meant the end, for all practical purposes, of the Ching dynasty. However, the dynamics had been changed. Public opinion in Europe and the United States turned against the policy of forcing China to accept an opium trade they clearly did not want, and by 1908 Britain and China had reached an agreement that allowed China to restrict opium imports.

Great Britain would probably be the closest comparison to the United States in terms of culture and, as in the rest of Europe, the use of opiates was widespread. Between 1831 and 1859, consumption of opium increased at a steady 2.4 percent per year (Booth, 1996, p. 51). In 1830, Great Britain imported 91,000 pounds of opium, and reexported 41,000 pounds, about half of it to the United States. By 1860, Great Britain was importing 280,000 pounds per year, and exporting 151,000 pounds.

In the United States, opium use also increased steadily throughout the nineteenth century. Some of this was due to increasing numbers of Chinese immigrants who brought their habit of smoking opium with them, and some was due to the American population joining them in their use of opium, but most of it was iatrogenic (inadvertently physician induced) (Perrine, 1996, p. 47). Physicians would prescribe opiates and many of the people who used them would become addicted. It is doubtful that the physicians themselves considered this a problem because, at that time, the opiates were not considered dangerous and few negative consequences existed for the addicted patient. Indeed, the largest group of white males who were using opiates were the physicians themselves. The most typical users, though, were white women, commonly middle class, who took patent medicines made of either opium or morphine in an alcohol base. These people may or may not have been addicted to opiates, and some of the use may have been for pseudomedical reasons, but it rarely interfered with their ability to function. Just as important, no social stigma was attached to such use.

It should not be concluded, however, that the widespread use of opium was without negative consequences. In fact, a number of social and medical ills were caused by the inappropriate use of opium. Interestingly, however, in both Great Britain and the United States, recreational use of the drug was relatively rare. Instead, it was used for both medical and pseudomedical reasons, and it was cheap and effective for the conditions treated.

Perhaps the most significant problem associated with opium and other narcotic substances was its use to control young children. Working mothers would use it to effectively treat diarrhea, various coughing ailments, such as whooping cough or tuberculosis, as well as cholera and other diseases of the gastrointestinal tract that were widespread; however, they also used it to calm demanding children, which allowed the mothers to sleep through the night. Inevitably, using opiates this way led to health consequences for the children. (It was also the drug of choice of mothers who euthanized unwanted children.)

This situation was what apparently prompted the 1868 Poisons and Pharmacy Act in Great Britain. This act restricted the sale of opiates by allowing only chemists (pharmacists) to sell it and required that every bottle carry a label stating the contents were a poison and displaying the skull-and-crossbones symbol. Initially, the act did what it was intended to do—by 1880 there was a significant drop in infant mortality in Great Britain. However, by 1900 it had climbed back to where it was prior to 1868 (Booth, 1996, pp. 64-65).

A distinction should also be made between those who used narcotics for medical reasons and those who used them recreationally. The latter made up a small group in the nineteenth century, and they even were the minority until nearly the middle of the twentieth century. Users who control their use and receive relatively pure drugs seldom have problems. Addicts who use impure narcotics and who do not control usage have profound problems. Consider this description of the addict who follows that spiraling path:

> The first symptoms of physical decline are inflammation of the mouth and throat, gastric illnesses and circulatory disorders which can weaken limbs so far as to paralyze them. . . . Quite often because of their constant physical lassitude and moral turpitude, they do not bother to take any interest in personal hygiene . . .
>
> As addiction deepens, the addict grows even more mentally and physically lethargic, lacking concentration and becoming forgetful. The body debilitates and becomes emaciated as appetite for food is lost: the voice grows hoarse, constipation develops with amenorrhoea and sterility in women or impotence in men. (Booth, 1996, pp. 88-89)

The author goes on to name a number of secondary complications that result from the miserable lifestyle that addicts typically lead. Two points are to be made here. The first is that although this occurred from time to time in the nineteenth century, it was quite rare among even those people who used morphine intravenously. The second is that most of the ills associated with narcotic addiction are due to lifestyle changes and are common to other forms of drug-addicted populations. That is, most of what the general public associates with narcotic addiction is a result of sociocultural factors, not that of narcotics per se. For example, if a typical person in the United States were asked to describe their image of a narcotic addict, they would probably describe someone with poor personal hygiene, slovenly in appearance, and as looking less than robust in health, and they would no doubt attribute all of this to the drug itself. It is unlikely they would describe a well-dressed person whose company might be desirable, and it is even less likely that someone such as their personal physician, a trusted professional, would come to mind as an example of a narcotic addict.

In contrast to this view, it is quite clear from a multitude of examples that if one has access to medically pure substances and sterile means of delivery, narcotics addiction is not debilitating either physically or mentally. Perhaps the most famous example of this is that of Dr. William Steart Halstead, one of the "big four" of Johns Hopkins University Hospital and a surgeon of impeccable reputation (sometimes called the father of modern surgery), who was a morphine addict from age thirty-four until his death at age seventy (Brecher, 1972).

One of the major players in the events that led to the eventual ban on narcotics in the United States was Hamilton Wright. In 1902 the United States acquired the Philippine Islands from Spain as part of the spoils of the Spanish-American War. Wright was named to the International Opium Commission and was a delegate to the Shanghai conference, which sought to control the international opium trade. This eventually led to the Hague Opium Conference in 1911. Wright was unalterably opposed to opium and morphine and used propaganda to promote his ideas. The tactics he employed may have even served as the model for Harry Anslinger and his famous campaign against marijuana, which produced such movie classics as *Reefer Madness* (1936).

At the start of the twentieth century, cocaine use was not considered much of a problem, at least when compared with opiates. Nevertheless, when the first legislation was proposed to limit opiates, this included cocaine. (This is how cocaine became defined as a narcotic by Congress.) Several good reasons exist for why cocaine should be a controlled drug. When abused, it produces a paranoid reaction. This reaction is indistinguishable from a psychotic state that results from a functional mental disorder, and it may take weeks to rectify itself after discontinuation of the drug. This aspect of cocaine was recognized as early as 1890, as was its addictive nature (Brecher, 1972, p. 275). Instead of depicting the true dangers of cocaine, to further his cause, Wright suggested that "negroes in the South were taking cocaine which put white women at risk, presumably from fornication" (Booth, 1996, p. 198). To understand why Wright chose this tactic, one must consider the culture of the time. To the public, this was both a believable and easily understood argument; understanding addiction was more difficult. When one cares more about a cause than the truth, factual presentations typically take a backseat.

In 1906 the Philippine Opium Investigation Committee reported its findings. These constitute Senate Document 265, read into the record of the first session of the 59th Congress. In terms of a useful document for Congress, 276 pages on the trafficking and use of opium in Japan, Formosa, China, Hong Kong, Saigon, Burma, Java, and the Philippines was probably too ambitious. The members of the committee were Edward Carter, Charles Brent, José Albert, and Carl Arnell. The Senate document called opium use "one of the gravest, if not the gravest, moral problems of the Orient." It was rife with racial bias, which was not surprising for the white men of the committee and the era in which it was written. Consider this statement about China: "There are no outdoor games in China or, indeed, any games in a gambling sense. Absolute dullness and dreariness seem to prevail everywhere. As these two demons drive the Caucasian to alcohol, so they drive the Chinese to opium." The report went on to state that the Chinese race may have reached a point in development at which the ability to be amused may have atrophied and disappeared (p. 29).

The committee recommended that only opium needed for medical purposes be brought into the Philippines, that the government should have a monopoly on its distribution, and that only males over twenty-one years of age should be given a license to use the drug (and that should be restricted to only those already addicted). They also said addicts should be given free hospital access for treatment for their condition. Foreigners who used opium illegally should be deported at the time of their third offense. Finally, the committee recommended that opium poppy cultivation should be made illegal in the Philippines.

The year 1909 brought the first federal regulation to narcotic drugs. President Theodore Roosevelt convened the Shanghai Opium Commission ostensibly in order to aid the Chinese Empire in dealing with their opium problem. To some degree, it appears to be political window dressing. The act was debated and passed as Public Law 221 while the Shanghai Commission was in session in February 1909. It was "an act to prohibit the importation and use of opium for other than medicinal purposes." In other words, its purpose was to prevent the importing of opium for use in opium dens. The debate on the bill (HR 27427) was notably brief. The bill was introduced by Sereno Payne of New York in the House of Representatives. Quick passage was urged so that the hand of the resident could be strengthened for dealing with the Shanghai Commission and its recommendations.

The only real objections to the bill concerned not the intent to ban opium smoking in the United States but whether the ban would have unintended consequences. In what today can only be described as ironically prescient, Representative Warren Keifer of Ohio worried the bill might have the effect of promoting manufacturing of opium in the United States and Representative Joseph Gaines of West Virginia suggested it might merely stimulate illegal imports (i.e., a black market). In the end, these arguments did not hold sway and the bill was passed without objection.

Other attempts to regulate the narcotics trade were introduced in Congress over the next five years, but without success. The first serious use of the law to limit narcotic use was passed in 1914.

THE HARRISON NARCOTICS ACT

Partly as a response to political pressures and partly as a result of fear of the spread of the Chinese drug problem, an act was introduced to the U.S. House of Representatives by Francis Burton Harrison of New York. It had the rather stilted title of "An Act to provide for the registration of, with collectors of internal revenue, and to impose a special tax upon all persons who produce, import, manufacture, compound, deal in, dispense, sell, distribute, or give away opium or coca leaves, their salts, derivatives, or preparations, and for other purposes." This act, introduced as House Resolution 1966 and passed as House Resolution 6282 by the 63rd Congress, became Public Law No. 223, effective December 17, 1914. For all practical purposes, despite a previous act that forbade the importation of smoking opium, this was the beginning of all federal regulation of recreational drug use.

Several authors have suggested that the intent of the act was merely to regulate trade and collect a tax. Brecher (1972), for instance, suggests such an interpretation. However, if you read the committee reports prior to the debate on the House floor and the debate itself, a very different picture arises.

In the report of the Committee on Finance (Ways and Means Committee, in Senate Reports, Vol. 1, of the 63rd Congress, 2nd Session on Senate Bill 6552, report #258, pp. 3-4), the debate decried the rapid increase of opiate use in the United States. In comparing the United States to Europe, it was noted that five European countries with a total population of 164 million used less than 50,000 pounds of opium annually. The United States, on the other hand, with a population of 90 million, imported 400,000 pounds per annum. Between 1870 and 1909, the population of the United States rose 133 percent, but opium use in the same period rose 351 percent. One senator noted in the record, "There has been in this country an almost shameless traffic in these drugs. Criminal classes have been created, and the use of the drugs, with much accompanying moral and economic degradation, is widespread among the upper classes of society." The basic goal of the report was to suggest that federal tax regulations be passed to support the various states so that the nonmedical traffic in opium could be reduced.

The debate on the House floor is even more instructive. This can be found on pages 2191 to 2211 of Volume 50, Number 3 of the 1913 Congressional Record. This was, after all, a tax act, so someone asked whether the purpose of the law was to raise revenue. Harrison answered, "The purpose of this Bill can hardly be said to raise revenue, because it prohibits the importation of something upon which we have heretofore collected revenue." It had been reported that in the previous fifty years the United States had collected $27 million in import duties on opium. Later, he added, "We are not attempting to collect revenue, but to regulate commerce." Representative Thomas Sisson noted, "The purpose of this Bill—and we are all in sympathy with it—is to prevent the use of opium in the United States, destructive as it is to human happiness and human life."

The bulk of the debate centered on two issues. One was the constitutionality of the methods being used to prohibit opium. Included in this debate was discussion of minutiae, but no dissension at all with the view that the intent was to eliminate the recreational use of opium was expressed.

The second issue that was debated concerned the medical use of opium. This was fueled primarily by Representative Sisson of Mississippi, who objected to a provision of the bill that called for personal attendance by a physician to receive a prescription for opium. Specifically, he was worried that it might require a physician to physically drive multiple miles to a rural location just to write a prescription for a patient whom he had already examined. What Sisson wanted was to change the bill's wording so that the physician could write refills without personal attendance on who he called the "unfortunates," the poor in his district who needed narcotics. The important point that came from this debate is that the medical use of opiates to support patients who were addicted to opium was clearly taken into consideration by the framers of the law. However, a disconnect existed between the apparent intention of Congress and the form implementation took. In what seems to be a monumental case of overzealousness, the Internal Revenue Service, which had the original responsibility here, determined that addiction was not an illness and that, therefore, physicians who prescribed narcotics to addicts were not in compliance with the act. Having nonmedical people make such a decision seems contrary to the intent of Congress, but court decisions later upheld this interpretation (see the next section).

Enforcement of the Harrison Act and Court Decisions

One of the first effects of the passage of the act was that addicts went to physicians for treatment. This led to another problem, because law enforcement had deemed that supplying addicts with narcotics was not allowed under the act.

The first case to reach the Supreme Court was that of the *United States v. Jin Fuey Moy* (1916). Moy was a physician who was reputed to have supplied "dope" to unregistered users. This case involved Moy giving 600 grains of morphine to an addict named Willie Martin. Because Martin was not registered under the provisions of the Harrison Act as someone who was allowed to sell morphine, then Moy was conspiring to violate the act by supplying him. The U.S. District Court of Western Pennsylvania had ruled against the government, and that ruling was appealed to the Supreme Court. The Supreme Court let the appellate court ruling stand, noting that "any person not registered" under Section 8 of the act "cannot be taken to mean any person in the United States but must be taken to refer to the class with which the statute undertakes to deal." In other words, mere possession of narcotics did not violate the act and, therefore, Moy could not be charged with conspiracy (Belenko, 2000, p. 69). If nothing else, this case exhibited the zeal that the government had for addressing narcotics addiction.

The more critical cases were those of the *United States v. Doremus* and the *Webb et al. v. United States,* both in 1919. In the Doremus case, a physician in Texas had supplied a known addict with a very large quantity of heroin. The government brought a case against him on the theory that, since the addict was not a licensed dealer, it was possible the addict would redistribute the drugs and not pay the proper tax on them. An appellate court quashed the original indictment, but the Supreme Court overruled it and reinstated the indictment, noting that the government had the power to levy taxes and collect fees. Hence, without being specific, the court seemed to suggest that prescriptions for large quantities of narcotics would violate the act unless those prescriptions were written for a person who was licensed under the act.

The Webb case involved a Memphis, Tennessee, physician who wrote prescriptions for addicts just so they could maintain their habits. The basis for the indictment and conviction was that since Webb merely supplied narcotics to addicts who requested them, this was outside the scope of the medical-practice exceptions to the law. The opinion of the court, written by Justice Day, was that such prescriptions did not meet the standards of medical practice. He wrote, in part, that "to call such an order for the use of morphine a physician's prescription would be so plain a perversion of meaning that no discussion of the subject is required." The Harrison Act had contained clear language to protect the practice of physicians and even contained debate on the floor of Congress that would seem to ensure that physicians would not have this kind of problem. Yet it was the decision of the Supreme Court that the law could be interpreted to mean that physicians could not prescribe narcotics just to maintain an addiction. This would have the effect of drastically reducing addicts' chances of finding a physician willing to prescribe narcotics for them. In effect, it was the first step toward building a viable black market in narcotics.

Still more cases were referred to the Supreme Court. They challenged the constitutionality of the law and the interpretation of Section 2, which dealt with what constituted "in the course of his professional practice only." In 1920, just one year after the Webb case, Jin Fuey Moy was once again before the bench. This time, though, the decision went the other way and the court seemed to reverse itself.

This indictment against Moy describes a situation in which the defendant was clearly prescribing morphine to addicts for the sole purpose of maintaining their addiction. This time the court became quite specific about what might constitute professional practice regarding narcotics. It noted that the immunity granted by Congress to physicians did not extend to "distribution intended to cater to the appetite or satisfy the craving of one addicted to the use of the drug." It further noted that a prescription for such purposes protects neither the physician nor the pharmacist who fills it.

This new interpretation was affirmed in *United States v. Behrman* (1922). The court did admit that "to prescribe a single dose or even a number of doses, may not bring a physician within the penalties of the act." However, this was a case in which the physician went so far beyond the bounds of common sense that even a layman would know that his actions were not within the bounds of professional practice. Here, a single patient was prescribed the equivalent of 3,000 doses of morphine. Nevertheless, Justice Oliver Wendell Holmes dissented. Since a jury had not been asked to judge whether the physician was overprescribing, Holmes deemed it beyond the scope of the judiciary to put arbitrary limits on what a physician might prescribe.

The general effect, of course, was to make it virtually impossible for a physician to prescribe narcotics to addicts. Law enforcement again attempted to push this interpretation to the maximum. This is apparent in *Linder v. United States* (1925), in which Dr. Linder prescribed one morphine tablet and three cocaine tablets to a patient known to be addicted. This is vastly different from the Behrman case, of course, and the court took note of this difference. The Harrison Act, for all its intent to bar the use of narcotics, was nevertheless a tax act, and one predominant theme in other cases was that supplying addicts high-dose prescriptions increased the risk that the addict would sell or transfer some of his or her narcotics without paying the proper taxes. After reviewing other cases, the court noted that the patient was not likely to sell or distribute the drugs supplied to her; therefore, this would not imperil the ability of the government to control narcotics and collect revenue from the sale of them. Linder was exonerated.

It would seem that the Linder case should have opened the door for physicians to challenge law enforcement's use of the Harrison Act to interfere with how they treated their patients. However, despite this decision, not many more cases entered the court system. Why would they? Physicians might disagree with the legal establishment, but it is difficult to believe that many would feel strongly enough to risk their professional practice or their freedom. According to Belenko (2000,

p. 98), the Nigro case in 1928 was the last to challenge the constitutionality of the Harrison Act. Thus, we have a situation in which Congress, law enforcement agencies, and the courts have joined forces to define an area of medical practice, although it is likely that few if any of these people had any professional credentials in the field of medicine.

Positive and Negative Outcomes from the Harrison Act

To some degree, whatever benefits the Harrison Act may have produced are speculative. It is very difficult to say what would have happened to opiate use in America had the legislation never been formulated or had it not been interpreted to include medicine. One very likely outcome from this act was a large reduction in the number of opiate addicts in the United States. Merely making something illegal, even with little or no attempt at enforcement or penalties, is typically enough to generate significant compliance. Opiate addiction was already waning from its peak around 1900, but it seems quite likely that its prohibition would enhance that trend. Another likely outcome might have been preventing the development of opium smoking dens as a common practice in the non-Chinese populations. Perhaps its biggest success was curtailing indiscriminate use of opiates and opiate-containing patent medicines for pseudomedical reasons. All of these outcomes were envisioned by the framers of the law, and one could hardly argue against their value. However, unanticipated and unwanted outcomes also developed.

First, when the law went into effect, a drastic drop in actual usage occurred. But, who stopped using? According to Lindesmith (1965, p. 21) only 18 percent of narcotics users were in any way involved in criminal activity, and that 18 percent included cocaine users. In other words, 82 percent of opiate users were ordinary, law-abiding citizens. Palfai and Jankiewicz (1997, p. 378) reported that the U.S. Department of the Treasury was inundated with requests for registration permits so that users could legally receive the drug. Few or none were actually issued. Thus, to a large extent, the people who stopped using opiates were not criminals or outcasts of society. They were typically productive members of society (Hanson and Venturelli, 2001, p. 230) who, because opiates became illegal, abided by the law and stopped using them. It is from this group of persons that you find the highest compliance. Some, no doubt, continued efforts to obtain morphine and some even turned to crime to support their no-longer cheap addiction, but most simply accepted the situation and found ways to stop. The real target of the act—hardened narcotics addicts who already committed crimes to support their habits—were not nearly so compliant.

Testifying on the Porter Amendment (see next section), Dr. Amos O. Squires, chief physician of Sing Sing Prison in New York, noted that in 1917 drug addiction of convicted felons was not much of a problem, with 0.4 percent of the new prisoners involved. However, by 1922, 9.1 percent were addicted, and 96 percent of these were addicted to heroin. This was another change; prior to the Harrison Act few heroin users were actually criminals. Instead, the typical user was a healthy, white, urban male between fifteen and twenty-five who preferred snorting the drug rather than injecting it. However, with the new restrictions on morphine requiring it to be smuggled into the country, and with the more compact nature of heroin making it easy to smuggle, the use of heroin increased rapidly (Palfai and Jankiewicz, 1997, p. 378). Neither the nature of the crimes nor the number of prisoners changed much over that time period. This lends support to the idea that the new laws had created a new class of addict—a criminal class. Interestingly, the recidivism rate for all prisoners was 54 percent, whereas the recidivism rate for the addicts was around 50 percent. In other words, it was not addiction that was sending people to prison, even though addicts were committing crimes to obtain their drugs. Those people would very likely have wound up in prison regardless of their addiction.

More important, where would an addict obtain narcotics if they were no longer available by prescription? The black market would be the only realistic source. This would lead to large profits from the nonmedical sale of narcotics, and with a captive clientele that market would flourish.

Thus, although the Harrison Act did address some social issues and did have positive outcomes for those issues, it also created new social problems that seem unlikely to have developed had this act not been passed. In the latter half of the decade following its passage, the act appeared to cause a net social gain; but that assessment becomes much more problematic when we look at the following decades.

THE PORTER AMENDMENT

The basic purpose of the 1924 Porter Amendment was to eliminate heroin. Specifically, it sought to prohibit the importation of opium into the United States for the purposes of manufacturing heroin. The hearing (held on HR 7079) exhibited a pattern that will continue throughout the history of acts and resolutions dealing with drug abuse. Testimony was presented to the committee both supporting the restriction and opposing the amendment, but the invited experts were in favor of it, and they denigrated the qualifications of those opposing it.

The first testimony was written input from Dr. Alexander Lambert. To a large extent, the testimony seemed accurate with regard to heroin, although it did contain a suggestion that heroin destroyed the "herd instinct" much faster than did morphine and that the so-called herd instincts were "the ones that control the moral sense" (HR 7079, p. 4), which includes responsibility for your fellow man. Hence, addicts would commit crimes with no sense of moral wrongdoing. Lambert did a credible job of explaining that cocaine was far more injurious to a person than was heroin and that heroin was just a stronger version of morphine. Previous testimony from William McAdoo, chief city magistrate for New York, had indicated that 98 percent of addicts were heroin users, and that those using only morphine or cocaine were rare enough to attract attention when they were discovered. McAdoo followed, though, with a description of two young men just back from Mexico who were addicted to heroin. It included gratuitous descriptions of their attire and of a "tan of a southern sun superimposed over pallid and emaciated faces, giving them a very sickly appearance" (p. 5). It was also noted that it was very easy to import heroin illegally, by concealing it in furniture, false suitcase bottoms, and hollow canes. The testimony revealed it was even readily found in prisons.

Unfortunately, subsequent testimony was much more problematic. Dr. Charles Richardson was invited to testify as a representative of the Executive Committee of the Board of Trustees of the American Medical Association (AMA). He noted, for example, that

> Heroin contains, physiologically, the double action of cocaine and morphia. It provides the excitation of cocaine with the sedative effects of morphia. It is more agreeable to take; it is not

followed by the nausea, as is so often caused by morphia, nor the marked depression afterwards. (p. 11)

He went on to denigrate the qualifications of an otologist (ear specialist) opposing the bill who had written to the committee, suggesting that no good otologist would use heroin. (Richardson had appeared to suggest no painkillers were needed for ear abscesses.) Another physician wrote in opposition of the bill. Richardson suggested that this was because he was from Pennsylvania, where three large drug-manufacturing companies were located (pp. 13-14). Richardson, a physician, in his testimony proudly boasted to the committee that he had never used heroin in his practice, that no competent physician needed it, and that other physicians who opposed the bill were either incompetent or had ulterior motives. He, by any objective standards, also displayed a notable ignorance of the effects of the drug.

The testimony of another invited physician was even worse. Dr. Rupert Blue, former Surgeon General of the United States, who was then working for the U.S. Public Health Service, stated that the drug did not cause constipation (as do other opiates) and, in addition, suggested that it was poisonous and produced insanity: "Undoubtably there are persons made insane by the use of these poisonous drugs" (p. 38). Many other statements were read into the record by various persons favoring the bill. Perhaps the most reasonable were those of Squires, the chief physician of Sing Sing Prison. He also suggested that the medical profession did not need heroin but, unlike Drs. Blue and Richardson, did understand the effects of the drug. It is likely that some of this came from his dealing with addicts as they entered his prison. The alarming part of his testimony involved the rapid rise in the use of heroin.

Given the testimony, Congress had no qualms about passing the measure, thus outlawing heroin in the United States. Would the legislation have passed had they been given only accurate information? Quite possibly, it would have. A fairly strong undercurrent existed in the country that was antinarcotic and antiheroin in particular. This also helps explain the continued insistence on laws that we now know from a better informed perspective likely do more harm than good. Those who make the laws are often exposed to both accurate and inaccurate information. Under such circumstances it becomes very easy to accept the testimony of people who match what you already believe and reject testimony that runs counter to your own biases or those of your constituencies. This is a theme that will be repeated often.

CREATION OF THE FEDERAL BUREAU OF NARCOTICS AND APPOINTMENT OF HARRY J. ANSLINGER

Administration and enforcement of both alcohol prohibition and the ban on narcotics were nested in the Department of the Treasury, but with two different divisions. The enforcement of the Harrison Act was originally the responsibility of the Bureau of Internal Revenue. The Federal Narcotics Control Board was initially under the direction of Levi Nutt, who held that post until the administrative structure was revised in 1930. In that year the Federal Bureau of Narcotics (FBN) was established and Harry J. Anslinger, who had been working in the alcohol prohibition area, was appointed the commissioner. This appointment was to have a profound significance in terms of how America viewed drugs.

Few or no other federal officials have been more unalterably opposed to recreational drug use than Anslinger. It was his zeal and his vision that would guide drug policy for the next thirty-five years. He held the post until he resigned in 1962, possibly due to pressure from the Kennedy administration (Palfai and Jankiewicz, 1997, p. 379). During this time period he showed he was willing to use any tactic, fair or foul, to fight the use of any narcotic drug. He continually pressed Congress for more and more stringent responses to drug offenders. His story is depicted in more detail in Chapter 3.

Chapter 2

Narcotics and Narcotic Regulations from 1937

The next major change in narcotic laws in the United States came with the Marihuana Tax Act of 1937 when marijuana* was added to the list of banned narcotics. Marijuana, though, presents a picture completely different from cocaine or the opiates. First, it is a mild hallucinogen that is not physically addicting as are the opiates. It also has a low psychological addiction potential, unlike both the opiates and cocaine. Physically, extensive use probably results in harm to the body that is equivalent to tobacco and, as with tobacco, it is likely its damage results in a statistically shorter life span rather than doing damage to body tissue (which can quickly be fatal). Psychologically, it produces an altered sensorium and slowed reflexes, making it dangerous to use while operating machinery or driving. However, it certainly does not drive its users insane and does not cause them to commit violent acts. It was not in widespread use in the first quarter of the twentieth century, although its use had begun to spread by 1937. Naturally, this is not how the drug was presented to Congress.

Dr. David Musto (1972) published one of the best reviews of the history leading into the Marihuana Tax Act of 1937. He also discusses an interview he had with Harry Anslinger in a commercial tape made by The History Channel (Musto, 1998). According to his review, although some minor pressure for the government to restrict marijuana had always existed, no one saw it as much of a problem. This even extended to Anslinger himself, who noted: "We weren't having any trouble with it" in his interview with Musto (1998). Several states, mostly in the Southwest, did pass antimarijuana legislation prior to 1937, but the new FBN was not yet concerned. In the

---

*The common spelling for the drug today is "marijuana," and that will be used throughout except when referring to a direct quote or to the specific name of the act.

1932 annual report to Congress, marijuana was considered nothing more than an inconsequential nuisance (McWilliams, 1990). If marijuana as a drug was not a major problem, why all the pressure to pass antimarijuana legislation?

As is often the case, a simple, one-rationale answer is not sufficient, but one factor that appears to be obvious is racial prejudice. Up until the mid-1920s, the great majority of users were people of Mexican heritage in the Southwest. Later in the decade, its use appeared to spread into the black and less-affluent white populations of several large cities, and it was associated with jazz music. Thus, its use was associated with certain ethnic groups, none of which were seen as desirable by the people in power. In particular, its use was associated with the Mexican laborer and, given the economic hardships of the Depression years, the American people of the Southwest resented their presence. They applied considerable pressure on their congressional representatives to do something about the Mexicans in the region. This yielded, among other things, Mexican repatriation in the 1930s, and generated a series of lurid newspaper stories about the evils of marijuana. This highlights another player in the drama—William Randolph Hearst.

Hearst was a publishing giant in the 1930s and 1940s and began a campaign in his newspapers to denounce marijuana. His reasons for doing so are unclear, but it has been proposed that it was done to protect his holdings in the paper industry (Herer, 2000). The hemp plant is an excellent source of fiber for pulp paper products. With the invention of a decorticating machine, the cost of raw materials for producing paper from hemp was roughly half the cost of producing it from trees. Since Hearst had large holdings in the wood pulp paper industry, hemp posed a serious financial threat. Was this the real reason Hearst joined the battle against marijuana? It is probably impossible to say for sure, and the actual reasons behind his campaign are probably not important anymore. What is important is that he controlled the content of a number of important newspapers and he used that leverage to spread antimarijuana propaganda. Hearst's newspaper holdings were impressive and included the *San Francisco Examiner* (from 1887), the *New York Morning Journal* (1895), the *Evening Journal* (1896), the *Chicago Examiner* (1902), and the *Boston American* (1904). He also owned magazines, including *Cosmopolitan* and *Harper's Bazaar.* At its height, his readership extended to 30 million readers and his fortune to $220 million, much of which was lost in the Great Depression. The classic film *Citizen Kane* is a fictionalized account based on Hearst's life.

The Mexican laborer, regardless of whether he or she was a legal immigrant, was an easy political target in the southwestern United States. Consider this quote by Roy Garis presented to the Texas legislature in 1930 (Ybarra, 2004):

> [The Mexicans'] minds run to nothing higher than animal functions—eat, sleep, and sexual debauchery. In every huddle of Mexican shacks one meets the same idleness, hordes of hungry dogs, and filthy children with faces plastered with flies, disease, lice, human filth, stench, promiscuous fornication, bastardy, lounging, apathetic peons and lazy squaws, beans and dried chili, liquor, general squalor, and envy and hatred of the gringo. These people sleep by day and prowl by night like coyotes, stealing anything they can get their hands on, no matter how useless to them it may be. Nothing left outside is safe unless padlocked or chained down.

As shocking as this description is today, it was likely an accurate representation of public opinion in 1930. Thus, if one could tie marijuana usage to this population and further suggest that the drug caused the people to become crazed and violent, it would be very easy to generate political pressure to control the evils of marijuana. This is quite similar to the tactic that had already been used to generate public sentiment against opium by tying its use to the Chinese.

Belenko (2000, pp. 137-146) reports a number of documents that, taken as a whole, both tie the use of marijuana to the Mexican laborer and purport to show the horrors of the drug. Among them are a quote from a Texas police captain in 1923 in which marijuana users were depicted as angry, violent, fearless, insensitive to pain, and possessing a "blood lust"; a newspaper report calling marijuana an "insanity-producing narcotic"; a 1927 *New York Times* article suggesting a widow and her four children had been driven insane by marijuana with "no hope of saving the children's lives and that the mother will be insane for the rest of her life." Also included are lengthy extracts from a magazine article written by Harry Anslinger and reporter and writer Courtney Cooper detailing similar propaganda. Because the drug was not widely used outside of small segments of the population, it was easy for the public to believe that marijuana really was an evil, killer drug.

The Marihuana Tax Act of 1937 bears a striking resemblance to the Harrison Act of 1914. It would have been easy to just add marijuana to the Harrison Act, but separate legislation was considered necessary because the plant was grown locally (for its fiber and seed). Since the Harrison Act and the Porter Amendment were concerned with importation of opium and coca leaves, the FBN thought that independent legislation was required. The mechanics of the measure were designed around the 1934 National Firearms Act, which had been used to control access to machine guns.

The Marihuana Tax Act sought to control the use of the drug by requiring a license and a transfer tax on all commerce involving it. As with both the Harrison Act and the firearms legislation, the stated purpose of the bill was to raise revenue through taxes, although the actual purpose was to restrict the actual use of the product. Producers of marijuana (presumably for fiber and seed) would be licensed at $5 per year regardless of acreage, dealers for $3 per year, and practitioners (such as doctors) for $1 per year. However, a tax of $1 per ounce would be imposed for each transfer of marijuana between licensed persons. The fee for unlicensed transfer was $100 per ounce. This figure was supposed to discourage the transfer of marijuana for purposes of smoking it. "Marijuana" was defined as the flowering tops, leaves, and seeds; fiber from hemp and sterilized seed were exempt from these transfer taxes. Control over recreational use, therefore, could be effected not only by making it prohibitively expensive for licensed persons to transfer it, but also by simply *not issuing* transfer stamps.

As happened with previous legislation, when Congress held hearings on marijuana a good deal of inaccurate information was presented. In this case, the information was blatantly false and, in all likelihood, knowingly so. Much of this false information came directly from the Federal Bureau of Narcotics. It is also interesting to note that the commercial farmers of hemp realized that legislation was being considered about their crop only at the last minute because they were unfamiliar with the term "marihuana," which appears to have been a localized name for the drug in the Southwest.

In the Senate hearings on HR 6906 on July 12, 1937, Clinton Hester, the assistant general counsel of the Treasury Department, testified on the effects of smoking marijuana cigarettes. The price quoted for marijuana cigarettes was twenty-five cents each—a price that appeared to astound Senator James Davis. Hester stated:

> Inhibitions are released. As a result of these effects, many violent crimes have been and are being committed by persons under the influence of this drug. Not only is marihuana used by hardened criminals to steel them to commit violent crimes, but it is also being placed in the hands of high-school children in the form of marihuana cigarettes by unscrupulous peddlers. Its continued use results many times in impotency and insanity. (p. 6)

This was followed by statements by Anslinger, who suggested that the intellect of young people who smoked marijuana was so damaged that they committed murder, robbery, and rape. In one particular case, he suggested a single marijuana cigarette was sufficient to develop a state of homicidal mania. He also noted that marijuana was not needed by the medical field.

It is also interesting to note that both Hester and Anslinger testified that no extra personnel would be needed to enforce this new act. The rest of the testimony was from representatives of commercial enterprises that used hemp fiber or seed for business. None of them objected to the efforts of the government to control narcotics, but many objected to the $5-per-producer fee, noting that a farmer with very small acreage was paying a disproportionate share of the tax.

The only testimony given not in support of this bill was by William Woodward, the legislative counsel of the AMA. It was presented on May 4, 1937, to the House Ways and Means Committee. In general, the AMA executive board was not in favor of an absolute ban on marijuana since it was still possible that valuable medical uses could be found for this drug. Woodward noted that nothing about the medical use of cannabis had any relationship to cannabis addiction. Among the more interesting points he made was that the committee was not relying on primary evidence to judge the issue. Instead, they heard testimony referring to newspaper accounts of the prevalence of marijuana addiction and its link to crime; they were not presented with any evidence from the Bureau of Prisons to confirm a link to crime. They heard testimony that schoolchildren were using marijuana, but did not receive any testimony from the Children's Bureau or the Office of Education to confirm it. The Division of Pharmacology of the

Public Health Service was not contacted for primary information about the effects of cannabis, and the Bureau of Mental Hygiene, which had control of the narcotics farms (such as the one at Lexington, Kentucky, as described in Chapter 7), had no record of any cannabis addicts ever having been committed to treatment facilities. The end result is that the committee failed in its responsibility to seek out the best information.

Finally, Woodward noted that forty-six out of forty-eight states already had laws for the control of marijuana. This would suggest that perhaps no need for new federal regulation existed. He provided the committee statements to that effect from the surgeon general of the Public Health Service in 1932 and from the U.S. representative to the League of Nations.

Questioning by the committee then began. The members of the committee were not gentle in their probing. They spent some time referencing a paragraph published as an editorial comment in the *Journal of the American Medical Association* trying to ascertain whether it was a quote from Anslinger or an editorial opinion, something Dr. Woodward was unable to answer. He was then harangued on whether he personally supported Title VI of the Social Security Bill of 1934, which sought to authorize spending $10 million to support research and public health works. The position of the AMA on the topic was not of interest to Representative Fred Vinson; he wanted to know why Woodward had not been before Congress to support the Social Security Bill and whether he supported that now. He was then pressed on why he did not support the Harrison Narcotics Act.

Woodward's response demonstrated a substantial level of insight to the problems of narcotics regulation. It is worth quoting here (in part):

> We [the AMA] favored it [the Harrison Act] to the extent of actively cooperating in the framing of it and securing its passage. We did not regard it as an act that was going to accomplish what it set out to accomplish; and it has not. If you will stop for a moment to think that the addicts of the country are still obtaining their supply of narcotic drugs through the drugs that are illicitly brought into the United States in contravention of the provisions of that act and that they distribute them in contravention of the provisions of that act—if you will examine certain testimony given by the Commissioner of Narcotics before the Judiciary

Committee of the House . . . cited in this very hearing as evidence in support of this bill, you will find that there is no such support at all but is a frank confession on his part that he needs more authority before he can enforce the Harrison Narcotic Act. (HR 6906, p. 105)

He then added: "you would find the enforcement of this act a thousand times more difficult than the enforcement of the Harrison Narcotic Act." The objection to the act, then, was on two grounds: The first was that marijuana might yet be found to have therapeutic value in medicine and the second was that the act would prove too difficult to enforce at the federal level. However, even as he decried lack of primary evidence, Woodward did not object to the avowed goal of the act of controlling a dangerous drug. He even went so far as to agree under questioning by Representative A. W. Robertson that it was an evil, habit-forming drug.

Despite this admission, he was then further subjected to intense questioning, which can only be described as the committee bickering over details. The tone is easily discernable as adversarial in nature. This is perhaps best illustrated by the fact that he was not thanked for his testimony, which is in stark contrast to all other witnesses before this committee and virtually any other testimony given prior to or since before such committees. Instead, the chairman merely announced the next witness. Whether this discourtesy had more to do with the specific testimony or with the fact that Woodward had been the spokesman for the AMA (which had fought with Congress over a number of other issues) is not easy to assess. It is quite possible both factors played important roles. No other witness testified against passage of this act. As a result, the committee received very little accurate information about marijuana.

The Senate and House both passed the bill with virtually no debate. One interesting incident took place when the Senate questioned the House concerning an apparent lack of input from the AMA. This is reported in the Congressional Record of July 26, 1937, on pages 7624-7625. The reply to the Senate was "Dr. Wharton [*sic*], representing the American Medical Association, testified at length." This was probably a reference to Woodward. If so, it was certainly disingenuous in that it left the impression that the AMA was in favor of the bill. In any case, once again, antidrug laws were passed not after careful consideration of the true aspects of the drug in question, and not with much understanding of long-term consequences, but in ignorance.

OPIUM POPPY CONTROL ACT

In 1942, Congress passed the Opium Poppy Control Act. This act required people to be licensed to raise opium poppies in the United States. The stated purpose of the act was to regulate trade of domestically produced opium that might be necessary in times of war. Prior to this poppies were grown not to produce opium, but to produce ornamental plants and seeds, which were used in foods or for decorations. The actual result of the act, though, was that it banned the growing of opium poppies in the United States.

THE BOGGS ACT

By 1950 it was becoming obvious that the efforts to control narcotics traffic were not working. The basic strategy had always been that of interdiction, meaning control of the problem could best be achieved by imposing fines and jail terms for those using or trafficking the drugs involved. Hence, if control was lacking, the obvious solution was to increase the levels of penalties. Prior to the Boggs Act (1951), no minimum penalty existed and all maximums were set at five years. Its passage established minimum and maximum penalties for possession or sale of narcotic drugs. Specifically, it set a maximum fine of $2,000 and a minimum sentence of two years for a first offense and five years for subsequent offenses, with maximums of five years and ten years, respectively. A $2,000 fine in 1951 would be the equivalent of approximately a $15,350 fine in 2005.

Representative Sidney Yates, testifying before the House Ways and Means Committee on April 7, 1951, stated there were 50,000 dope addicts, mostly of the "criminal type" whose moral fiber had been destroyed. Because of this, "victims of dope, like victims of smallpox, must be quarantined for their own protection and for the protection of the rest of society" (p. 41). Since only 1,187 convictions were recorded in 1949, if Yates's estimation is correct, then the arrest-and-conviction rate of addicts was only 2.3 percent. This did not seem to disturb Yates, but the fact that two-thirds of them received sentences of under two years did. He went on to depict examples of the evils of "dope" and suggest that the situation had become so serious that judges should no longer have any discretionary power for second and third offenses. Other congressmen gave similar testimony, suggesting that mandatory sentencing guidelines were needed.

George Cunningham, deputy commissioner for the Bureau of Narcotics, provided some comparison figures from other crimes. For those convicted under the White-Slave Traffic Act (also known as the Mann Act) which was directed at preventing interstate prostitution, 19 percent were placed on probation and 9.3 percent received sentences of more than five years. In comparison, of those convicted of narcotics crimes, 25 percent received probation and only about 3 percent served sentences of more than five years. Cunningham then went on to confirm that the white slave trade had for the most part ceased, and this was attributed to the stiffer sentences imposed (p. 68). He compared Memphis, Tennessee, to New Orleans, Louisiana: In New Orleans the typical sentence was one year and one day; for the same offense, the typical sentence in Memphis ranged from five years to fifteen or eighteen years and, according to Cunningham, "you just aren't going to catch dope peddlers in Memphis" (p. 69).

In the end, over the course of three days of hearings, the committee heard testimony from fifteen individuals. This generated more than 100 pages of text on the issue of opiates, cocaine, and marijuana. (Barbiturates and amphetamines were also considered, but since they are not "narcotics" they lie outside the scope of this work.) A significant portion of this testimony related to the use of narcotics (mostly heroin) by teenagers and schoolchildren. All of the testimony was consistent in suggesting that narcotics could only be controlled, and would in fact best be controlled, by longer prison terms and more severe fines. To use a common phrase, the testifiers were preaching to the choir. The Boggs Act passed Congress with virtually no debate.

NARCOTIC CONTROL ACT OF 1956

This legislation had two significant thrusts. The principal one was to provide harsher penalties; the other was to broaden the laws on marijuana specifically. The act had several other provisions as well, including making search warrants easier to obtain. During the hearings, the House and Senate had some significant differences regarding the bill.

The provisions of the bill called for a sharp increase in penalties for using or dealing narcotics. The Boggs Act (mentioned earlier) provided for a minimum two-year sentence to a maximum five years for first-time violators. This rose to five to ten years for second offenders and ten to twenty years for those who offended more than twice. No distinction was made between dealer or user, and judges were allowed discretion in terms of probation or early release. The persons convicted and sent to prison were treated no differently from other prisoners in terms of parole. The new bill left the previous penalties according to the Boggs Act intact for users, but for dealers selling to an adult, the first-time offender faced a five-year minimum sentence with a twenty-year maximum, and all subsequent convictions carried a ten-year minimum with up to a forty-year maximum. If the sale was to a minor, the first offense produced a ten-year minimum sentence with up to a forty-year maximum. Possible fines rose from a maximum of $2,000 under the Boggs Act to a new maximum of $20,000. Finally, if the seller was over eighteen and provided narcotic drugs or marijuana to someone under eighteen, he "may be fined no more than $20,000, and shall be imprisoned for life, or for not less than ten years, except that the offender shall suffer death if the jury in its discretion shall so direct" (Section 107 [i]). To ensure that these penalties were actually imposed, judges were barred from using discretion in sentencing and could not permit a suspended sentence or allow probation.

In explaining the need for this change, the government seems to have relied more on intuition than hard evidence. On one hand, they extolled the Boggs Act's harsher penalties for improving the situation. At the same time, they noted that the situation in terms of illegal drugs entering the country was deteriorating. The House Committee report (#2388 for 84th Congress, Second session) began by noting the evils of addiction. This report also defined addiction as having three elements: a compulsion to use the drug, a need for increasing dosages, and psychological and sometimes physical dependence. Since marijuana was not singled out but was instead grouped with the other drugs, it was included as an addicting agent. Unfortunately, the report went on to state: "Drug addiction is not a disease. It is a symptom of a mental or psychiatric disorder" (Representative Boggs, p. 8).

It was estimated that the United States had about 60,000 addicts (a rate of 1 out of 3,000 adults), that the average an addict spent on his habit was $10 a day, and that this translated into an estimated $219 million per year spent on illegal narcotics. Yet the situation was perceived as improving, based on arrests. The report stated the peak year for arrests was 1952 (no statistics were given), with decreases to 23,627 in 1953 and 19,489 by 1954. The implication was that the more severe penalties provided for in the Boggs Act were having an impact; hence, it is only logical to assume even harsher penalties would have a greater impact.

The report also considered the possibility that the narcotics should be legalized and their distribution controlled by the government. Responding to this notion, Boggs suggested that narcotic drug addiction served no useful purpose. He went on to say: "There can be no justifiable reason for its continuance. To permit a governmental institution to engage in the ghastly traffic in narcotics is to give the government the authority to render unto its citizens certain death without due process of law" (p. 67).

In the Senate hearings (Report #1997), rather than suggesting the situation was getting better, the committee seemed to imply it was getting worse. Just as the House relied on arrests to estimate the level of illegal narcotics use, the Senate relied on seizures at the port of entry to estimate that the amount of narcotics entering the country was increasing sharply. The report suggested that the country had "little hope of stemming the increased flow of drugs into the United States" until Congress passed heavier penalties (p. 4). Trying to put the rationale from these two reports together into a coherent whole is no easy task. On one hand, we learn that the situation is getting better because we have harsher penalties. However, it is also getting worse due to trafficking and we need even harsher penalties to reverse the trend. In both cases, relying on the effectiveness of your agents in terms of arrests or seizures only works if no other elements change.

In the case of seizures, when you examine the actual numbers between 1945 and 1955,* a strange pattern emerges. A steady and significant drop in opium seizures occurred between 1945 and 1951 (622 pounds to 56 pounds); then a drastic surge in 1952 (up to 462 pounds) another steep fall in 1953; and a steep rise in 1954. Heroin

---

*Hearing before the subcommittee on improvements in the federal criminal code of the committee of the judiciary, United States Senate 84(2) Congress, May 4, 1956.

seizures were more variable but held fairly steady from 1948 to 1951, only to increase sharply in 1952 (237 percent increase), and massive seizures of cocaine occurred in 1948 and 1949 compared with other years. Marijuana (both domestic and nondomestic) showed this same peak in 1949. Clearly several factors must have played a role here—especially between 1951 and 1952—since the demand for these drugs couldn't have fluctuated that much. This is partly explained by changes in the agencies themselves. Ralph Kelly from the Bureau of Customs, testifying before this subcommittee concerning a sharp increase in seizures in the first eight months of 1956, noted that they had added new agents and new border check points in the Southwest, gave border agents and immigration agents equivalent powers of arrest, added new equipment (two-way radios), paid more money to informers, and changed training. Although no record of wholesale changes in procedures in previous years exists, it is still a more parsimonious assumption that changes in seizures are more likely due to personnel and technique than to changes in demand or the actual flow of drugs. It is also quite likely that as soon as an agency improves its procedures those smuggling and distributing drugs will adjust their routines and methods.

The call for harsher penalties was not universal. One dissenting opinion was provided by Deputy Attorney General William Rogers. Testifying before the Senate committee, he noted that increasing the penalties for trafficking may cause greater resistance to prosecution and make convictions more difficult to obtain (foreshadowing Samuel Walker's "law of criminal justice thermodynamics," which is covered in Chapter 5). He went on to note that since penalties were a matter of legislative policy he concurred with the longer sentences, but he urged that discretion in applying them not be removed from judges. David Kendall, acting secretary of the Treasury, also questioned the desirability of the drastic increases in penalties. He noted, for instance, that juries were unlikely to impose a death penalty on an offender.

The other significant provisions of the act related mostly to marijuana. This act widened the scope of the law with regard to transportation of marijuana such that a person could be prosecuted in any venue, not just the state in which the transfer of the drug took place. It also specifically prohibited marijuana smuggling specifically rather than relying on the general smuggling statutes, and allowed the use of wiretap information in drug prosecutions. Finally, it also required any person convicted of a narcotic drug offense in either a state or federal court (including addicts) to register with the U.S. Customs Service if they wished to cross the United States border. Since the customs agents had the power of arrest without warrant and the right to conduct body cavity searches, the result of this provision would be that anyone known to be a user would likely be subjected to an extensive search upon returning to the United States.

Although not part of the act itself, testimony on the act revealed that a significant change in the views of the Bureau of Narcotics was occurring. Testifying before a 1955 Senate subcommittee investigating illicit drug traffic, Anslinger noted that the marijuana addict is not a true addict (Belenko, 2000, p. 147). This was a major change from the position maintained consistently for the previous eighteen years. Under questioning from Senator Price Daniel, Anslinger proposed what would become the "gateway" theory of narcotic addiction. He suggested that marijuana use over a long time period would lead the user to heroin addiction. Did this mean the government was ready to reconsider its stance on the nature of marijuana? Consider this exchange:

> [Daniel] "Is it or is it not a fact that the marihuana user has been responsible for many of our most sadistic, terrible crimes in this nation, such as sex slayings, sadistic slayings, and matters of that kind?"
>
> Mr. Anslinger hedged: "There have been instances of that, Senator. We have had some rather tragic occurrences by users of marihuana. It does not follow that all crime can be traced to marihuana. There have been many brutal crimes traced to marihuana, but I would not say it is a controlling factor in the commission of crimes." (Lindesmith, 1965, p. 230)

Here Anslinger is not quite giving up the position that marijuana is linked to violent crimes, but he is not stressing the link as stridently as he had done in the past.

NARCOTIC ADDICT REHABILITATION ACT OF 1966

By 1966, a significant, although not dramatic, shift of thinking about what to do regarding the narcotics problem occurred. This may or may not have been related to the retirement of Harry Anslinger. The number of addicts in the prison population continued to rise to more than 57,000 in 1965. Many of these were addicts who had previously been in prison for drug-related crimes; however, between the years 1956 and 1965 an average of about 7,350 new addicts each year appeared. Especially among the latter group, some were in prison only for possession, not for sale or other crimes. Rather than group these people together with all of the other prisoners, Congress passed an act that would allow for treatment for addicts in lieu of prison. If the person was deemed "likely to be rehabilitated through treatment," they could be civilly committed for confinement and treatment of their problem rather than put through the federal prison system.

For the purposes of this act, an addict was defined as any person who habitually used any narcotic drug. The addict was required to decide within five days of his or her indictment whether he or she wished to enter the treatment program. The court could then mandate an examination period of up to sixty days for the surgeon general or attorney general's office to determine if the person fit their profiles and, if so, the addict could be remanded to the custody of the surgeon general for treatment. The maximum allowable course of treatment was thirty-six months. If the addict left the program, or if after thirty-six months the surgeon general could not certify that the addict was "cured," then criminal proceedings would resume. Otherwise, the criminal proceedings were quashed. This would seem to be a risky proposition for the addict, except that the thirty-six months of treatment would be credited toward any prison term he might receive.

The program also was made available to addicts who were not charged with any criminal activity if the United States attorney determined that state or other treatment facilities were not available to the person. That is, an addict could turn himself or herself in for treatment. However, in doing so, the addict was placing himself or herself into the custody of the surgeon general and could not back out of the program. The commitment would be court ordered and, the way the act was written, had the potential to be indefinite with recurrent six-month hospital stays. This likely would be enough to give most addicts second thoughts about the desirability of such a program. However, another category of addict existed. A relative of an addict could petition the court for this program. In this case, the alleged addict could be ordered to appear before the court for an examination and in the end suffer an involuntary civil commitment.

The passage of this act had several positive aspects. Primarily, it offered addicts an opportunity to deal with their addiction specifically rather than merely serve a prison sentence, which may or may not offer legitimate treatment. To this extent, this act was a more enlightened approach to the problem. It was also funded by Congress at $15 million per year. On the downside, the program's availability was not an entitlement; the court had the final say on whether an addict was offered this option, and it would be quite rare for it to be offered to someone who was involved in criminal activities of any kind. Furthermore, while an outlay of $15 million is laudable, it was also woefully inadequate to treat the numbers of new addicts entering the system, let alone the repeat offenders. Still, it was a positive step.

Within three years, the situation changed again. Dramatic shifts in attitude culminated in a complete overhaul of the federal regulations in 1970.

COMPREHENSIVE DRUG ABUSE PREVENTION AND CONTROL ACT OF 1970

This act started as the Controlled Dangerous Substances Act of 1969 and is now typically referred to as simply the Controlled Substances Act. The committee reports leading up to the passage of the act contain some remarkable statements. In Senate Reports 91(1)-613, a report by Senator Thomas Dodd from the Judiciary Committee clearly considered marijuana separate and distinct from the other controlled substances. For the first time since the passage of the Marihuana Tax Act, due notice was taken that this drug problem was not as serious as that of cocaine or opiates. The report went further, no longer classifying it as a narcotic drug. It even suggested harm was being done by prohibiting marijuana, noting that marijuana laws have contributed to alienation of youths since they considered the laws hypocritical. In the introduction to the bill itself, Senator Dodd's report contained the following:

> To impose the same high mandatory sentences for marihuana related offenses as LSD and heroin offenses is inequitable in the face of a considerable amount of evidence that marihuana is

significantly less harmful and dangerous than LSD or heroin. It has also become apparent that the severity of penalties including the length of sentences does not affect the extent of drug abuse and other drug-related violations.

Consider that second sentence; it has profound implications. It suggested that harsh sentences and mandatory prison terms do not curtail the traffic or use of controlled substances. This is an absolute reversal of the long-standing position of Congress.

It should have been clear that harsh and mandatory sentencing was not solving the drug problem. Despite the passage of the 1956 Narcotic Control Act, drug-related arrests had continued to rise. Dodd's report noted that between 1960 and 1968 the number of arrests per year had grown by 322 percent. In one year alone, between 1967 and 1968, a 64 percent increase in arrests occurred. The report went on to suggest that penologists believed mandatory sentences hampered the rehabilitation of offenders.

By 1970 this bill, passed without opposition in the Senate, had been changed to the Comprehensive Drug Abuse Prevention and Control Act, which subsumed all previous drug-control legislation and made dramatic changes. It changed the definitions used for important terms, changed the sentences imposed for violations, established schedules of drugs that are still in use today, established a new federal agency to oversee all aspects of illicit drugs, and eliminated the practice of trying to control dangerous substances by resorting to tax codes.

According to this act, a drug-dependent person is someone who uses a controlled substance and who is in a state of psychic or physical dependence (or both) arising from the use of that substance on a continuous basis. Hence, the concept of addiction is not tied to any specific drug or set of drugs. A drug abuser is anyone who uses any controlled substance in a way that violates the law. Drug-related offenses include any crime a person commits to obtain the drug, whether directly or through money raised by the crime, and any crime committed while under the influence of a controlled substance. The most significant definitional change was that of a *narcotic*. Under Section 102(16), a narcotic is defined as any form of an opiate or cocaine. Marijuana is not included; it is defined separately under 102(15).

This act also established the schedules of drugs, called Schedule I through V. The drugs listed were specific but the listing also included any isomers, esters, ethers, or salts of the specific banned drug as well as any salts of the isomers, etc. The original list contained eighty-one drugs broken down by opiates, opium derivatives, and hallucino- genics. Listing drugs this way made it possible to still produce a "de- signer" drug that was chemically distinct from the original but that still had the same efects. Drugs classified under Schedule I were com- pletely criminalized in the United States. These drugs were cited for having a high potential for abuse with no accepted medical use. In the listing of specific drugs are several specific opiates, such as heroin. However, not all opiates are included. Other drugs that were on Schedule I included marijuana preparations, sedatives such as metha- qualone, and a number of psychedelics, including lysergic acid die- thylamide (LSD), peyote, psilocybin, and others. To be removed from this schedule and placed in a different category would require an act of Congress.

Schedule II drugs would be available only in limited quantities un- der a physician's treatment. This group included the opiates other than heroin, such as morphine and codeine, cocaine, and amphet- amines. Schedules III, IV, and V include controlled drugs with less potential of abuse, for which physicians could write refillable pre- scriptions. In some instances (e.g., codeine), whether a drug was con- sidered Schedule II, III, or V depended on the amount used. Some substances in Schedule V were even available without the physician's supervision. These included very limited quantities of codeine in cough syrups.

The other major change brought about by this act was the removal of minimum sentences for drug offenders. It also distinguished be- tween marijuana and the narcotics by imposing lighter sentences for sale or transfer of marijuana than for cocaine or heroin. Lighter sen- tences were also mandated for simple possession of all controlled substances. The only offense that did have minimum sentencing was "continued criminal enterprise." This was a provision for people who were involved in organized crime—supervisors or managers of at least five other people who were making profits from illicit drugs. The one seemingly anomalous quirk in the new guidelines involved age-related offenses. To be charged as an adult, a person needed to be at least eighteen years old. However, he or she was still a minor until age twenty-one. Since sale or transfer to a minor carried a double maximum penalty for a first offense, if the seller sold drugs to someone who was older than him or her, but who was also a minor, he or she faced a double penalty. Unfortunately, as we will see, this trend toward lesser penalties did not last.

COMPREHENSIVE DRUG PENALTY ACT OF 1984

This act amends Section 511(a) of the Controlled Substances Act of 1970. This section provided for seizure of properties of persons involved in illicit drug-trade activities. Any person engaged in illicit activities that yield profits is subject to forfeiture of all properties obtained from such activities. This act streamlined the process so the property would not need to be housed in a government compound for years at a time while the tedious paperwork process was finished. It did this by creating a "permissive presumption" that all property acquired by a drug offender during the period of violations or shortly thereafter was subject to forfeiture if no other likely source existed for such property. This meant, for example, that if a person attempted to smuggle drugs via a boat and was intercepted, the government could seize that boat and sell it—all within a few months.

The other provision of the act dramatically increased the monetary penalties a court could impose, typically by a factor of ten. If the original ceiling for a monetary fine were $25,000, this act raised that to $250,000. The rationale presented for this was that the profits in drug trade were so high that dealers considered a fine of $25,000 just part of ordinary business expenses.

CONTROLLED SUBSTANCE ANALOG ACT OF 1986

This act filled a significant hole that had developed in the capacity of the government to keep up with changes in the drug underworld. Using the schedule of drugs developed in the 1970 Comprehensive Drug Abuse Prevention and Control Act, if someone "invented" a new drug by chemically altering an existing drug, or formulated an entirely new drug, that new substance (called a "designer drug") would have to be put through the process of getting it listed on the schedule of drugs. Because this was a relatively lengthy process, this meant it was temporarily legal to possess that drug on the street. The Analog Act added the proviso that if the new or altered drug produced substantially the same effect as a drug that was already scheduled, the new drug automatically was placed at the same schedule level. Thus, if someone produced a substance that had the same basic effect as heroin, that new substance was automatically a Schedule I drug and banned at its inception.

ANTI-DRUG ABUSE ACTS OF 1986 AND 1988

Just two years apart and with the same name, these two acts were both designed to address the so-called war on drugs. Crack cocaine had been invented in 1983 and had risen to the top of the public agenda. A flurry of newspaper and magazine articles about this new menace appeared. A CBS documentary, *48 Hours on Crack Street,* was the most widely watched documentary in television history with 15 million viewers (Belenko, 2000, p. 306). The legislation passed in 1986 provided $1.7 billion dollars in new spending, mostly directed at interdiction efforts, and substantial increases in penalties for the sale of drugs. At the same time, it lessened penalties for mere possession. First offenders could be sentenced to rehabilitation rather than prison or even probation and, even with two prior convictions, the individual might receive as few as ninety days. On the other hand, a judge could also sentence a first offender to up to a year in jail and a fine of $1,000 to $5,000, with jail time and fines escalating upon subsequent offenses.

Another provision of the 1986 act was to ban possession of drug paraphernalia, which could be used to take marijuana or tetrahydrocannabinol (THC)-containing products, phencyclidine (a dissociative anesthetic typically classified as an hallucinogen), cocaine, or amphetamines. A number of other provisions were covered in the legislation (which was 192 pages long), but the overall thrust appears to be one of returning to harsher penalties.

Two years later, it was more of the same. The 1988 act went even further than the 1986 act regarding harshness of penalties. This act was also mainly concerned with crack cocaine. A person who merely possessed five grams or more of cocaine base was subject to a mandatory five- to twenty-year prison term at the time of his or her first offense! The sentence for a third offense was life without parole; this was a mandatory sentence. For possession of less than five grams, one could be fined up to $10,000. In the case of a drug-related homicide, both perpetrators and abettors could receive the death penalty.

This was not the end of this type of legislation. For instance, the Crime Control Act of 1990, another of those omnibus kinds of acts that covers a lot of territory, in effect was merely a continuation of policies already in place. The cornerstone of the federal response to drug abuse remained the imposition of harsh penalties. With no really significant changes occurring since the 1980s, let's skip forward to the present.

CURRENT FEDERAL SENTENCING GUIDELINES

The actual sentencing guidelines are too complex to reproduce in full or in an appendix. The handbook for determining these can be found online in PDF format at <http://www.ussc.gov/2003guid/2003guid.pdf>. Drug-related offenses not involving other crimes are broken down into two categories: trafficking and simple possession. The guidelines begin by sorting offenses into levels by amount of the drug involved. The base level of penalty obtained can be altered by any of a number of other factors, such as if weapons were involved or if death resulted. Once that base level has been obtained, a second factor is criminal history. This system yields an allowable range of sentence, with the width of that range determined according to a formula.

For drugs, the maximum base level is 38 if no other crime is involved. This level is reached by selling a huge quantity of drugs, such as 30 kg or more of heroin, 150 kg or more of cocaine, etc. As the amount sold decreases, so do the penalties. They go down to a minimum level of 12 (for selling five grams or less of heroin). If the offense is mere possession, the level of offense can range anywhere from 4 to 8. According to this system, selling less than five grams of heroin warrants a minimum sentence of ten to sixteen months (under the best of circumstances), and selling 30 kg or more would net from about twenty to twenty-four years for a first offense. The odds of being caught with a sale of that magnitude for the first time (zero criminal-history points) would seem rather small, however. At the opposite end of the spectrum, being arrested for mere possession of heroin could result in a penalty range of anywhere from zero to six months.

The end result has been a burgeoning prison population. In a January 4, 2004, airing of the CBS show *60 Minutes,* Ed Bradley reported that prison populations had increased from 43,000 inmates in 1987 to 173,000 in 2004 at a cost to taxpayers of $4 billion per year. In these days of huge federal budgets, this amount seems almost trivial. However, it could still be used in a more efficient manner than by just warehousing more and more people caught trafficking or using illicit drugs. Also, this figure represents only the difference between mandatory sentences and judicial discretion, and not the entire cost of incarcerating drug offenders.

WHAT DO JUDGES THINK?

The difficulty with the sentencing guidelines is that they remove a great deal of judicial discretion. The concept was to make sentencing more uniform and to ensure that potentially dangerous people are not released without proper retribution. However, by using this system, we tie the hands of those people who should be in the best position to actually adjudicate what penalty should be meted out. The reality is something very different. Judge Harry Edwards of the DC Circuit, U.S. Court of Appeals, notes (in *United States v. Harrington*) that sentencing guidelines merely shifted the discretion from judges to prosecutors, something he calls "gamesmanship." A prosecutor could, for instance, decide to apply or not apply any of several sentencing factors such as selling drugs near a school zone or to a minor. He or she could allege the defendant was a ringleader. This gives prosecutors leverage to gain cooperation from the accused, but it also means the same crime will not necessarily produce the same sentence even when the guidelines are applied. Edwards went so far as to label the guidelines "a bit of a farce."

A good general summary is that judges are not much enamored with the federal sentencing guidelines and mandatory sentences. Judge Jack Weinstein of the U.S. District Court, Brooklyn, New York, stated in 1993: "As a judge, in the 80's and 90's, I have become increasingly despondent over the cruelties and self-defeating character of our war on drugs" (*New York Times* op-ed, July 8, 1993). Judge Robert Pratt of the U.S. District Court, Southern District of Iowa, goes somewhat further in his description. Noting that the concern of disparity in sentencing in the federal system is a legitimate one, he also suggests that moving to a mandatory sentencing system has not addressed the real problem, saying, "What have we done by creating a system that many federal judges have rejected as unfair, inefficient and, as a practical matter, ineffective in eliminating drug use and drug-related crime" (*Des Moines Register,* January 10, 1999). Pratt also noted that 86.4 percent of district judges thought the mandatory guidelines should be altered, and 70 percent favored repeal of almost all mandatory sentencing.

An even stronger statement was made by Judge Stanley Sporkin speaking at a symposium on the tenth anniversary of these sentencing guidelines in Washington, DC, on September 9, 1997:

> We are filling our jails with a lot of secondary violators of the drug laws. Recently, I was told that under the sentencing guidelines, I would be required essentially to sentence a drug addict to a ten year period of incarceration. If this person were from a different socio-economic background, he would have gone to the Betty Ford Clinic for 60 to 90 days. As I contemplated the sentence I would have to impose, all that came to mind was a modern day version of *Les Miserables.*
>
> There is one case where I had to sentence a 49 year old woman to 21 years in prison for selling $25 worth of crack to an undercover officer. . . . In another case, a defendant faced a 30 year sentence for selling 6.7 grams of crack to an undercover officer to whom the seller was attracted for the wrong improper purpose. I was able to pare the sentence down to about seven years but even that was too long. This individual was as much a threat to society as my eight year old grandson.

The problems the mandatory sentencing guidelines were designed to address were real. In the judiciary were both liberals and conservatives and good judges and bad judges, depending on whether you were a defendant or a prosecutor. A punishment for committing a crime really should not depend on where a person is tried in federal court or the personality of the judge a person appears before.

Even more troubling is that the sentences for the enfranchised populations were typically more lenient than those for the disenfranchised. To put it bluntly, a white thirty-year-old male with no criminal record would probably receive a more lenient sentence than a black thirty-year-old male with no criminal record who committed the same crime. Since these guidelines were formulated at a time when the United States was moving toward harsher penalties, they were more aimed at ensuring the white male was treated just as severely as the black male. But did they really work that way? See Chapter 5 for further analysis.

Chapter 3

Agencies of Enforcement

At the inception of the drug laws, no special agencies to deal with violators were set up. The original legislation was, theoretically, a tax act; therefore the federal agency responsible was the Bureau of Internal Revenue nested in the Department of the Treasury. In 1927, a new bureau, the Bureau of Prohibition, was established. It also was part of the Department of the Treasury, and took on the responsibilities that formerly belonged to the Bureau of Internal Revenue. This change was really just an internal reorganization.

The first major change occurred in 1930 with the creation of the Federal Bureau of Narcotics (FBN). This too was part of the treasury department; however, this reorganization was mandated by Public Law No. 357 of the 71st Congress on June 14. It provided for a commissioner of narcotics to be appointed by the president and for a deputy commissioner to be appointed by the secretary of the treasury without regard to civil service laws. This would open the door for appointment of people for ideological reasons rather than demonstrated competency. With the establishment of the FBN, Congress also named a new Division of Mental Hygiene under the direction of the surgeon general (which office is also in the Department of the Treasury). This division would oversee patients placed in the recently mandated narcotic farms. This established a working relationship between the office of the surgeon general and the commissioner of the FBN.

The first person appointed to commissioner of the FBN was Harry J. Anslinger. Similar to J. Edgar Hoover of the Federal Bureau of Investigation (FBI), Anslinger would establish what was, for all intents and purposes, a personal empire. From his position, he would wield great political power in the area of narcotics and dangerous drugs. Considering the enormous impact Anslinger had, it seems reasonable to investigate what kind of person he was.

Two excellent sources of information about Anslinger and his tenure can be found in McWilliams' (1990) biography, *The Protectors,* and Gray's (1998) book, *Drug Crazy.* They paint very different portraits of the man. McWilliams view is so positive it is almost apologetic; Gray's view is equally negative. McWilliams points out that Anslinger was actually involved in much more than just the FBN and its operation. Besides his role in directing the FBN, Anslinger was involved in the nascent intelligence community that had ties to the Office of Strategic Services (OSS), which later became the Central Intelligence Agency (CIA); he was involved in pushing the FBI to recognize the role of organized crime, in particular the Mafia; and he was instrumental in building international agreements concerning the drug trade. Anslinger is often depicted as monolithic and a martinet, but in fact he was an exceptionally talented bureaucrat who is perhaps better compared to an evangelist on a mission than to a troglodyte. His motives and his policies may be questionable, and the kindest description of his tactics may be that they were unacceptable, but his political skill and passion were impeccable.

Anslinger originally worked for the Pennsylvania Railroad, where he was instrumental in stopping an insurance fraud claim. He managed this by attending to details and doggedly rooting out the facts, something the local police apparently failed to do. He must have achieved considerable personal satisfaction from this first instance of police work as well as from it reflecting on him favorably as an employee. It was also during this period of time that he overheard Italian laborers talking about the "black hand"; this was probably how he became concerned about organized crime. Beginning in 1918, Anslinger worked in the diplomatic corps for the United States and was stationed variously in Germany, Venezuela, and the Bahamas. In the Bahamas he distinguished himself by getting the British more involved in preventing alcohol smuggling. Up to this point he was not really involved in regulating narcotics or other drugs, but was working full-time on alcohol prohibition. In the meantime, the chief of the Narcotics Division of the treasury, Levi Nutt, was involved in scandals that made him a liability. Hence, when it was time to appoint the new commissioner of the FBN, an opening was just waiting for Anslinger. It probably didn't hurt that the secretary of the treasury, Andrew Mellon, was related to Anslinger by marriage and had appointed him as acting commissioner. President Hoover made it permanent on September 23, 1930. This appointment lasted until his retirement in 1962 and spanned administrations ranging from conservative to liberal. According to Galliher, Keys, and Elsner (1998), writers for decades have marveled at the success of Anslinger in not only keeping that post but in his ability to use law enforcement to control public opinion about recreational drugs. Part of this was the political power he wielded by maintaining support of the Women's Christian Temperance Union, many churches, and the drug companies themselves (since these drug companies had to work through Anslinger to get licenses to produce narcotic drugs). However, his real genius was in linking illicit drugs to minority populations, thus feeding on racial prejudices.

Very early in his career, Anslinger manifested the seriousness with which he took violations of the drug laws. Even before his appointment with the FBN he had written a paper suggesting how Congress could more effectively implement the Eighteenth Amendment (McWilliams, 1990, p. 33). In this treatise he proposed mandatory penalties of fines and imprisonment for illegal purchasing of alcohol starting at $1,000 for a first offense (a very heavy price when this was written in 1928, especially when this fine was proposed for a speakeasy patron buying one drink) and escalating to as much as $50,000 for subsequent offenses, including a two-to-five-year jail term. This reliance on severe sanctions would remain one of his hallmarks throughout his career. According to Gray (1998), Anslinger never gave up on prohibition, remaining convinced that all one had to do to make it work was increase the penalties sufficiently.

ANSLINGER IN CHARGE

Anslinger himself wrote a book published in 1964 with the title *The Protectors*. It is about the activities of the FBN and its agents. One would think this would give some insight into the man's thinking, but in fact it tells very little. One of the most remarkable passages from that book is that "Prohibition, by depriving Americans of their 'vices,' only created the avenues through which organized crime gained a foothold" (pp. 10-11). This is as close as he ever came to admitting that prohibition may have had some undesirable results. He appears to have continued to believe alcohol prohibition was the morally correct course to take even if it did cause problems.

Still another interesting connection is the long arm of Hamilton Wright. His widow, who had accompanied her husband to the 1912 Opium Conference in the Hague, continued crusading against opiates after his death, even serving as a delegate to the 1925 International Opium Conference. She apparently wielded significant political power. She visited Anslinger shortly after his appointment as commissioner. She must have liked what she found, as she lobbied for Anslinger and the FBN afterward. Anslinger considered her help with Congress invaluable.

Long before 1932, considerable pressure to repeal alcohol prohibition existed. The election of President Franklin D. Roosevelt and the dramatic political change in climate that occurred with it sealed the fate of prohibition, and the Twenty-First Amendment became law. Anslinger suggested that it was predictable that organized crime would turn to the narcotics trade, ignoring the fact that they were already involved in narcotics trafficking. In his book he reported that "addiction was on the rise again" and that people were being addicted "unknowingly" (p. 21) as they were introduced to criminal circles. He connected the narcotics trade to white slavery. Everywhere he looked, he saw evil perpetrated in the name of narcotics. His attitude toward narcotics and illicit drugs is quite obvious in his book, but his motives are obscure.

Harry Anslinger will be most remembered for his activities in successfully lobbying for federal regulations banning marijuana. By 1930, when he took over the FBN, a number of states had already banned marijuana, including Louisiana and California. Anslinger initially wanted no part in federal regulation. Not only did he believe that marijuana wasn't really a problem but also, according to Musto (1972), he was very worried about how his agency would go about controlling a substance that grew freely as a weed. Even after the passage of the Marihuana Tax Act, he warned his agents to stay focused on heroin, not marijuana, and if an agent made a series of marijuana arrests he was told to get back to "the hard stuff." This is actually very telling; it would indicate Anslinger knew very well that marijuana wasn't the horrible assassin of youth it had been made out to be, despite the vitriolic statements he made about it before Congress. In addition, he had other independent evidence that marijuana wasn't really a killer weed, including a communication from Dr. Michael Ball in 1937 attesting to the inaccuracies in the position of the FBN (McWilliams, 1990, p. 61). Finally, despite a later reversal on this issue, Anslinger himself testified before a Congressional hearing that no connection between marijuana and heroin existed.

So if Anslinger knew better, where did his opposition to the drug come from? It would have been helpful if he had discussed this in his own book, but it contains nothing whatsoever about this. Marijuana is barely mentioned at all, other than a bizarre story of a girl seduced by marijuana in 1948. It must be assumed, therefore, that what drove Anslinger was largely political in nature. And there is no question that politicians from the Southwest wanted federal control of marijuana. What motivated those politicians was pressure from their constituents and that, in turn, could be traced back to simple racial prejudice. All banned substances at one time or another were associated with some identifiable group of people who lacked political power or social status, and marijuana was no exception, as it was strongly linked to the Mexican laborer. With the Depression and many people out of work, the cheap, Mexican labor used for the fruit, vegetable, and cotton harvests was undesirable by most people. It took very little in the way of adverse publicity—publicity the newspapers were happy to supply—to turn people against marijuana.

The stories of the evils of marijuana started in the 1920s and depicted the drug as causing crazed, criminal behavior in the Mexican population. The stories most often originated with law enforcement personnel, but they also may have been generated by reporters or by zealots such as Earl and Robert Rowell, who waged a campaign against the "weed of madness" (King, 1972, p. 74). Newspapers were rife with accounts of its horrors and the Hearst chain gleefully sent the stories around the nation. Still, according to Musto (1972), Anslinger felt that Congress wasn't really enthusiastic about taking action, so, to ensure passage, he presented the case against marijuana in the strongest possible terms. Virtually the entire body of evidence he presented at Congressional hearings consisted of newspaper stories—stories that had no actual basis in fact. It seems quite likely that Anslinger must have known this, but making things up and presenting them as facts was a common tactic he used throughout his career. In any case, he was successful in steering the Marihuana Tax Act through Congress.

To get the act passed Anslinger had declared marijuana a national menace. Three years later he declared it under control (Gray, 1998, p. 81). This was common in the reports to Congress throughout his tenure: If you need numbers to support a particular view, just make them up. No one ever seems to have questioned them. For example, according to the FBN, white heroin addicts greatly outnumbered blacks, then suddenly, in one year's time, the reverse was true. Anslinger claimed the FBN's tactics had reduced the addict population of America from 250,000 to 60,000 or less, but he never stated exactly how he generated these statistics. When questioned about how he could provide such precise numbers such as exactly 7,172 addicts in Illinois, he replied, "Because within two years every addict will come to the attention of the authorities whether he's poor or rich" (Gray, 1998, p. 82). In other words, if a person wasn't arrested within a two-year time frame, almost by definition he or she wasn't an addict. The assailable logic behind that assumption appears to have gone unquestioned.

When the Red Menace reared up in 1949 with the fall of China to communism, Anslinger tied narcotic addiction to the communists, which succeeded in getting the FBN's budget doubled over the next five years. However, because drug use was increasing, especially in black and Puerto Rican sections of cities in the North, extra money and agents wouldn't be enough. This was used as the springboard to support stiffer penalties for narcotics. The result (with Anslinger's blessing, if not from his own devising) was the Boggs Act of 1951.

In the meantime, trouble concerning marijuana was on the horizon; the La Guardia Commission in New York was meeting. Mayor Fiorello La Guardia commissioned a panel to investigate marijuana in 1939 under the auspices of the New York Academy of Medicine. From today's perspective, it was an impressive report that actively refuted virtually all the myths that had been perpetuated about marijuana by the FBN and others. When the final report came out in 1945, the commission had found that marijuana was not a gateway drug (a position that Anslinger himself once held), did not cause addiction, was not in widespread use by children in school yards, was not related to juvenile delinquency or major crimes, and did not lead to aggressive or violent behaviors. Unfortunately, details of the report began to leak out while it was still a work in progress. Anslinger, with his position being undermined, began launching personal attacks on the members of the commission calling them "dangerous" or "strange" people (Gray, 1998, p. 83). He does not appear to have been interested that he had his "facts" wrong about the drug (and it's fairly obvious he knew that well before the La Guardia Commission went to work), but appears to have been motivated to prevent anything that would impinge on his area of control as commissioner of the FBN from happening. Marijuana was still widely feared by the public, and that served as a resource for the bureau. Anslinger's tactics were successful and the report had only a minor impact when it was released.

Using such tactics to denigrate the members of the La Guardia Commission was, again, the standard for Anslinger. He used the same tactics and worse to put down anyone else he perceived as an enemy of his agency. Among the most nefarious of these situations involved a Canadian film in 1946 titled *Drug Addict,* which was championed by Alfred Lindesmith. A full report of this conflict is contained in an article by Galliher, Keys, and Elsner (1998). Lindesmith was a young professor of sociology at Indiana University (IU) when he came to the attention of Anslinger. He publicly supported the World Narcotics Research Foundation (WNRF) and had published a report titled "Dope Fiend Mythology" in a law journal. Anslinger responded by informing IU that a "drug addict and a collection of racketeers" were among the sponsors of the WNRF and arranged to have a San Francisco judge write a rebuttal to his article to be published in the same journal. This was also a common tactic of Anslinger; he not only attempted to censor accurate research on the effects of drugs but also sponsored "research" projects that would support the FBN's positions.

The film *Drug Addict* was an award-winning Canadian documentary production that supported Lindesmith's views. It portrayed addicts as victims with a sickness rather than as drug fiends. It actually went overboard in this regard by not presenting much of the seamier side of the addict's life, but nevertheless it portrayed them more accurately than did the popular media. It noted that addicts and traffickers came from all walks of life and weren't restricted to specific races, that high-level traffickers were almost all white, and that law enforcement seldom targeted high-level dealers but instead concentrated on street-level dealers. It concluded that "Complete control of the traffic in drugs is impossible." This final conclusion was, of course, anathema to Anslinger, who based his whole rationale for being in the concept that with enough money and sufficiently harsh penalties he could wipe out illicit drug use. From Anslinger's point of view, this film was dangerous and challenged everything the FBN was saying; it had to be stopped.

Anslinger began by writing to the president of the Motion Picture Association of America (MPAA), Eric Johnston, telling him he would write to Canadian authorities urging the film not be made available in the United States because if shown there it "would do incalculable damage in the way of spreading drug addiction" (Galliher, Keys, and Elsner, 1998, p. 673). Indeed, in 1949, a representative of the Canadian government indicated to Lindesmith that Anslinger had made such a request. He even asked Canada to censor the film; this request was rejected. He then asked that no citizen of the United States be allowed to view the film in Canada, and this also was rejected. When Lindesmith received the backing of his congressman, who then contacted Anslinger, Anslinger replied falsely that the film had been banned under the motion picture industry's code. In the end, Anslinger was successful in preventing the film from being shown when other government agencies that might have been supportive did not have the temerity to cross the FBN.

The culminating chapter of this private vendetta by Anslinger against Lindesmith came in 1956 when Lindesmith managed to form the Joint Committee of the American Bar Association (ABA) and the Ameriocan Medical Association (AMA) on Narcotic Drugs, chaired by Rufus King of the ABA, to investigate the drug problem. The money that supported the commission's work came from the Russell Sage Foundation. This effort produced an interim report with a limited number of copies for internal distribution within the AMA and ABA. It was titled *Narcotic Drugs: Interim Report of the Joint Committee* and was not very favorable toward the FBN. The response of the FBN was a report published under the Department of the Treasury titled *Comments on Narcotic Drugs: Interim Report of the Joint Committee,* using the same cover and typeface. Unlike the original report, this one was widely distributed. It attacked the original and its authors, suggesting they had already made up their minds before the committee was formed. Anslinger then went after the Board of Trustees of the Russell Sage Foundation, using veiled threats regarding loss of their tax-exempt status and suggesting the report's authors had communist ties. This resulted in loss of funding for the commission.

Nevertheless, Lindesmith, serving as editor, managed to get the final report published by Indiana University Press in 1961, as *Drug Addiction: Crime or Disease?* Anslinger attempted to suppress this publication through the same kind of intimidation tactics he had used before. He had the FBN make inquiries of the IU Press regarding reasons for publication, whether any public monies were being used, how it was to be distributed, etc., although in this case Anslinger was unable to threaten them with loss of tax-free status if they published the report. Finally, when the report was published, rather than attempting to refute the facts and conclusions (which would have been logically impossible), the FBN produced a rebuttal report with the same name, format, and layout as the other report, apparently to sow confusion among readers. Perhaps as a result of Anslinger's tactics or other factors, Lindesmith's report seemed to have little or no impact. While all of this was happening, the FBN managed to virtually eliminate any reputable research about the drug by refusing to issue Treasury licenses to possess the drug to researchers. The number of Treasury-approved research projects peaked in 1948 with eighty-seven licenses given out, but dropped to eighteen in 1953 and only six in 1958 (King, 1972, p. 85). Once again, Anslinger had defended his turf using whatever tactics were necessary, and the ultimate loser was truth.

The Boggs Act of 1951 actually had little impact on drug addiction or illicit trafficking, so the next step was the Narcotic Control Act of 1956. As with the Boggs Act, Anslinger did not author the legislation or propose it, but he supported it in the hearings. Once again he tied the communist menace to illicit drugs, suggesting this was a common way for communists to undermine American democracy. Again, this is part of a pattern of "if you don't generate the results you want with a law, increase the penalties until you do." We will examine the fallacy of this line of reasoning in Chapter 4.

The final note on Anslinger's tenure at the FBN does have an element of poetic justice in it. It is not clear why he resigned in 1962, but it may have had something to do with Rufus King and the Lindesmith commission. According to Gray (1998), King had a series of public confrontations with Anslinger. In 1961, King was visited by an assistant to the White House science adviser, Jerome Weisner, who asked King for information on Anslinger. King presented the assistant with a tape of a debate that was broadcast on NBC Radio's *Monitor,* which was later played for President Kennedy in the Oval Office. The obvious implication is that this was what ended Anslinger's career, but no proof of this exists. McWilliams (1990), for instance, offered a very different scenario, including the fact that Anslinger had reached mandatory retirement age of seventy. However, McWilliams admits that the actual reasons for his leaving were unclear.

THE POST-ANSLINGER ERA

If Gray's (1998) assessment of why Anslinger retired is to be believed, then his replacement must have been somewhat surprising. Kennedy chose the FBN's Deputy Commissioner, Henry Giordano, who was Anslinger's closest associate and whose philosophy on drugs was virtually the same as Anslinger's. However, change for the agency itself would soon occur.

In 1965, a second agency, the Bureau of Drug Abuse Control (BDAC) was created. This was nested under the Food and Drug Administration in the Department of Health, Education, and Welfare. A Presidential Advisory Commission had recommended that the illegal traffic in amphetamines, barbiturates, and drugs of abuse other than narcotics and marijuana needed to be controlled. The BDAC was thus created for this purpose. The problem, of course, was that the government now had two agencies to control illicit drugs; it would be inevitable that their duties and areas of control would overlap. Another problem was that both agencies were dealing with the criminal justice system, yet neither had been originally designed for this.

The situation got even more complicated in 1968. The FBN and the BDAC were merged into a new department, the Bureau of Narcotics and Dangerous Drugs (BNDD), which was housed in the Department of Justice (DOJ). Moving to the DOJ certainly made sense, as did merging the two agencies in terms of what they were trying to control. What complicated matters was the creation of four more offices or agencies, two in the DOJ and two elsewhere, to go with the new BNDD. In the DOJ, to supplement the activities controlled in the BNDD, the Office of National Narcotics Intelligence and the Office of Drug Abuse Law Enforcement were created. In addition, the U.S. Customs Service retained an Office of Drug Investigations (under the Department of the Treasury). Finally, an Executive Office of the

President was created to contain the Narcotics Advance Research Management Team.

Common sense finally prevailed with the creation of the Drug Enforcement Administration (DEA) under the DOJ in 1973, an administrative structure still in place today. An excellent history of the DEA can be found online through their Web site (www.usdoj.gov/dea).

CURRENT REGULATIONS AND STRUCTURE

Although the basic organizational structure still remains, several significant changes have been made since 1973. One such change was the passage of the Drug Enforcement Coordination Act of 1984, which established the position of "Drug Czar," a position held today by John P. Walters. At the time, seventeen different agencies were involved in the war on drugs in some capacity. It was hoped that having one person oversee all these activities would result in better coordination and less wasted efforts or duplication. In 1988, the Anti-Drug Abuse Act established the Office of National Drug Control Policy (ONDCP), an office still in existence today. Interestingly, its subtitle for Section 5251 was "United States Policy for a Drug-Free America by 1995." The implementation of that policy appears to have had some limitations.

Several agencies were responsible for drug and alcohol treatment initiatives. In 1974, the Alcohol, Drug Abuse, and Mental Health Administration (ADAMHA) was created to supervise the activities of the National Institute of Drug Abuse (NIDA), the National Institute on Alcohol Abuse and Alcoholism (NIAAA), and the National Institute of Mental Health (NIMH). In 1992, the ADAMHA Reorganization Act abolished ADAMHA and generated a new supervisory agency, the Substance Abuse and Mental Health Services Administration (SAMHSA). The torturous route from the inception of the Division of Mental Hygiene in 1930 to treat narcotics addicts through all the various guises of agencies that culminated in SAMHSA is enough to give anyone but a history buff pause. The legislative history of the NIMH, for instance, can be found online at <www.nih.gov/about/almanac/historical/chronology_of_events.htm>. SAMHSA itself consists of three agencies or centers—the Center for Substance

Abuse Treatment (CSAT), the Center for Substance Abuse Prevention (CSAP), and the Center for Mental Health Services (CMHS).

Many agencies, each with their own budget and mandates, involved in some fashion or other the war on drugs. When we add up all the budgets of these groups, we get a final total of $19.18 billion for fiscal year 2003 (Federal Drug Control Programs, 2002).

On March 1, 2003, a new Cabinet level post, the Office of Homeland Security, was enacted. This office overlapped the functions of some other cabinet posts. For instance, the Coast Guard was transferred from the Department of Transportation to the Department of Homeland Security. The result of this reorganization makes it very difficult to compare funds spent on drug interdiction in 2002, 2003, and 2004. It is also important to bear in mind that these agencies don't deal only with illicit drugs such as heroin, but also with alcohol and tobacco, and with mental health issues. Rather than trying to sort all of this out with a verbal description, the various agencies and budgets for 2002-2003 are listed in Appendix I. That series is the source for the $19.18 billion.

The breakdown of this money offers some insight into governmental priorities. Dividing that $19 billion into the three broad categories of treatment, education, and interdiction, 19.9 percent is budgeted for treatment, 12.9 percent for prevention or education, and a whopping 67.2 percent (or more than $12 billion) for interdiction. Interdiction itself can be broken down into domestic law enforcement (such as catching the bad guys and putting them in prison), domestic interdiction (such as Coast Guard activities), and international interdiction (such as attempting to eradicate foreign production). Using this breakdown, we spend 49.3 percent of our budget on law enforcement, 11.9 percent attempting to intercept drugs at the border, and 6 percent trying to eradicate drugs overseas.

In fiscal year 2003, a major change in this structure occurred. This change was cosmetic rather than substantive, and may have been designed so that it appeared that relatively more money was being spent on education and treatment than in the past. Starting with fiscal year 2003, the antidrug budget no longer reflected expenditures for the consequences of drugs, which means the total dollar amount for the "War on Drugs" dropped by almost $7 billion. In a ONDCP circular (April 18, 2003, p. 7) explaining the changes, the issue was addressed this way:

The National Drug Control Budget, as restructured, does not include budget estimates associated with the secondary consequences of drug control enforcement. Funding for certain activities of agencies where drug control is incident to broader agency missions is also excluded from the modified drug budget.

It is not entirely clear what that means, as a budgeted item for treatment still exists. With this new way of looking at the budget money, even though the same dollars are being spent on the same items, starting in fiscal year 2003 we are spending 46.6 percent of the "War on Drugs" money for treatment and prevention (labeled demand reduction) and only 53.4 percent on the interdiction portion. This is disingenuous at best. The reality is that if we restructured fiscal years 2001 and 2002 budgets to match the new methods, the two-year average for demand reduction is 46.55 percent—no change. Now add in the changes that occurred as a result of forming the cabinet post for Homeland Security, and it becomes almost impossible to really compare the budgets between 2003 and 2002. The new structure, with its budgeted items, is presented in Appendix I.

What we have generated to this point, then, is an enormously complex web to administer and an equally complex set of laws. Someone once quipped that a camel is a horse designed by a committee. When the committee is Congress, the horse that emerges may not even bear much resemblance to a mammal. If it all worked—if we were winning the war on drugs—it would be worth it; but it doesn't work. This is a Rube Goldberg set of laws, which are often based on faulty premises and which do not meet the objectives they were intended to meet. What is strange about all of this is that acknowledgment that it doesn't work is widespread, but that recognition does not seem to generate much in the way of impetus to change present policy. We appear to be willing to keep the present policies and practices intact rather than try to fix them. For example, U.S. Attorney Paul Warner of Utah, recently testifying before a Senate subcommittee, stated:

> I believe it is both fair and safe to say that we will never prosecute our nation's drug problem out of existence. We have tried to do that since the 1960s and we have yet to succeed. Yet, I hasten to add that vigorous and aggressive criminal prosecution of illegal drug activity in our country should continue to remain as a

cornerstone of our National drug control strategy and policy. (U.S. Senate, 2001, p. 12)

This is a blatant admission that current policy won't accomplish the goal of eliminating drugs, yet Warner expressed a desire to continue down that same path because he was worried that legalizing drugs would "send the wrong message." Actually, as discussed in Chapter 8, good reasons to maintain the illegality of a number of recreational drugs exist, but this does not mean the current system should not be changed.

This is the politician's dilemma. There is no shortage of evidence that our present approach has not worked well; a number of examples demonstrate that this approach to illicit drugs does more harm than good. However, to change our policy would seem to many like a moral collapse—giving up to the forces of evil. This confusion between the moral intentions of actions and measured outcomes is a major barrier to be overcome. Chapters 4 and 5 discuss some of the failures of present policy and lays the groundwork for suggestions for revision.

Chapter 4

Interdiction As a Strategy

The constant struggle between drug enforcement agencies and illicit traffickers in narcotics and other dangerous drugs is not a zero-sum game. Every time the authorities change the rules or change their procedures the criminals will have a corresponding response. If interdiction begins to succeed in any one area, supplies will be routed from other avenues; if the total supply volume changes, prices on the street will also change to reflect that; if penalties for use or possession change, so will the specific activities of those selling and distributing the drug. The only reasonable goal of law enforcement using interdiction as a strategy must be one of containment rather than eradication, as eradication is simply not achievable. In other words, it's not necessarily a failure when narcotics continue to enter the country if the final level of consumption drops. It might even be termed a success of sorts if the consumption level merely remains constant, since the cry of enforcement agencies is that use would soar without their efforts or if the drugs were made legal. Unfortunately, even given this caveat, it becomes fairly obvious when examined that these efforts have yielded only very limited successes and, by many people's standards, have actually been failures.

Interdiction as a strategy has been the hallmark of efforts made in the United States to control illicit drugs from the beginning and remains the area in which we place most of our resources. Interdiction means stopping the flow of product to the user. Logically, you can break these efforts into three sequential parts: stopping the drugs at point of origin by destroying crops and/or on-site drug labs; stopping the drugs as they enter the country (smuggling activities); and stopping the drugs on the street by interfering with the importer-dealer-pusher-user chain of connection. We will look at all three of these areas, focusing first on heroin, on the smuggling aspect in particular.

HEROIN INTERDICTION

The advantages of heroin for use in analysis of interdiction strategy is that its production is entirely nondomestic and demand never drops. The government has kept statistics on levels interdicted at the borders since 1926, as well as estimates of levels of addicts. Unfortunately, curious gaps exist in these records and it is quite likely that the older data are simply not reliable. For instance, the number of heroin addicts through 1967 appear to be based on the number of persons arrested for dealing or using the drug and the number of addicts arrested for other crimes that enter the prison system. In other words, they are merely guesses and likely seriously underestimate the actual numbers. In order to use such data to analyze the problems, many assumptions must be made.

Look at the problem U.S. Customs has in monitoring goods and materials brought into the country. This description is from a DEA Web site:

> Each year, according to the U.S. Customs Service, 60 million people enter the United States on more than 675,000 commercial and private flights. Another 6 million come by sea and 370 million by land. In addition, 116 million vehicles cross the land borders with Canada and Mexico. More than 90,000 merchant and passenger ships dock at U.S. ports. These ships carry more than 9 million shipping containers and 400 million tons of cargo. Another 157,000 smaller vessels visit our many coastal towns. (http://www.usdoj.gov/dea/concern/drug_trafficking.html)

What a task! Heroin is among the more compact drugs that are smuggled and can be placed into clothing, concealed packets, hollowed-out furniture legs, body cavities—the list is endless. It should be obvious that without some magical device that can detect it at a distance, no realistic hope of ever stopping all that comes in exists. What is most discouraging is the very small proportion that we intercept. The classic, standard figure typically given is that 10 percent of illicit drugs get seized. Regarding heroin, even the government admits that estimate is optimistic. In a March 2002 report on heroin availability prepared by the Office of National Drug Control Policy as a Presidential Report, the official seizure estimate for heroin in 1996 was only 4 percent. It was 7 percent in 1997, 5 percent in 1998,

4 percent in 1999, and 6 percent in 2000. However, a little analysis and logic will demonstrate that even those miserable figures are probably optimistic.

Here's where it gets tricky. First, how many heroin addicts are there? Since addicts are engaged in an illegal enterprise, they will not always be forthcoming if asked whether they are addicts. The procedure used by the government to estimate numbers is complicated and arcane to say the least. They rely on answers to surveys such as the National Household Survey on Drug Abuse (NHSDA), arrest numbers, proportion of prisoners who are addicted, and mathematical formulas. We will use the official government figures, but it is all just guesswork. These guesses require we take so many variables into consideration that it is difficult to have any faith in them.

Second, how much heroin does a given addict use? Addicts will vary a great deal on this figure. It will depend on stability of supply, cost, purity, how long they have been using the drug (since use tends to be progressive), and method of using (snorting will necessitate a larger volume than injecting). Again, we must consider many variables. Still, spread out across large groups, some kind of statistical average or typical figure might be devised. The advantage of heroin compared to other drugs for this analysis is that addicts will insist on a steady supply and will use a relatively steady supply; no major changes occur, even across longer time periods. Hence, the total volume in use day by day across the United States should be relatively stable and relatively independent of short-term fluctuations in supply even though addict populations swell and recede (and a significant number will die each year due to their habit). The actual proportion change from year to year is never great, even when trends are toward greater or lesser use.

This can be demonstrated by taking three-year rolling averages to substitute for individual years. If we assume that new stockpiles of the drug are not being created, we can take those numbers and use them to get some idea of how much heroin is actually entering the country. We can't really depend on seizure rates to give us this figure because drug seizures are not like harvesting crops, during which you collect a steady amount. They're more like fishing; some days you catch a lot and some days you don't catch any. The logic is that if a specific addict needs X mg of pure heroin daily, that translates into $X \times 365$ mg a year. If we know how many addicts exist and if a typical addict is a reliable estimate of the average addict, then it is possible to estimate the actual total usage. That amount should be the *least* amount that must be getting through the border. Note that the estimate derived this way will actually be quite liberal in terms of total interdicted since it doesn't take into consideration dabblers who are using heroin on an occasional basis but who are not yet addicted; they also will be using some of the supply.

According to personal interviews, the typical addict in a large Midwestern city uses at least 200 mg of pure heroin daily. This figure was derived from using a street-level purity of 40 percent, a level that seems to fit well with other sources, the price on the street, and the amount the typical addict was reported to be spending to support his habit. However, this number seems high compared to some others. For instance, using the same methodology and the numbers from a 1994 ONDCP report, 75 mg per day would seem to be more realistic. Some addicts will use more, and some less; no attempt is made here to suggest any specific average amount of heroin used across the country or even per addict. It is all very problematic and unreliable. Still another complication comes from the variation in dosages a given addict might use. A maintenance dose (the minimum necessary to stave off withdrawal) is different from a dose to get high on. An addict who needs 100 mg a day to feel good might require 250 mg daily to have an enjoyable recreational experience.* Finally, because of the cost, users might supplement their heroin use with pharmaceutical opiates when they can acquire them.

Based on official figures (which are seriously suspect) from 1961 through 1967, we actually managed to interdict around 3.5 percent of the heroin entering the United States. (See Appendix II for a summary of these numbers). In more recent times, both the number of addicts and the amount of heroin seized have increased dramatically. The average number of hard-core heroin addicts from 1988 through 2000 is officially estimated at 849,769 (Johnston, Rhodes, and Carrigan, 2000) and the number is rising, with the year 2000 estimate of 977,000 users. On the other hand, the National Survey on Drug Use and Health (formerly called the National Household Survey On Drug Abuse) reported only 166,000 current (within the previous month) heroin users in 2002. These numbers are so discrepant that they clearly represent different counting methods or assumptions.

---

*Based on information collected at the Paseo Clinic in Kansas City, Missouri.

For purposes of this analysis, let's stay with the larger number. Between 1991 and 1998 the United States managed to seize an average of 1.3 metric tons of heroin per year. However, to service only the hard-core addicts would take more than 23 metric tons. The average is actually a 5.9 percent interdiction rate. Again, it bears repeating that since these numbers don't include dabblers, this is actually a liberal estimate. Furthermore, even official government estimates show the problem getting worse. In 2001 the ONDCP published its annual report, which suggested only 650 kg (0.65 metric tons) of heroin was seized at the border, and also estimated that 13.05 metric tons made it into the country. Thus, using these numbers, the rate of interdiction was only 4.7 percent, but using an estimate of 27 tons required (based on 2000 figures), that would be only 2.4 percent successfully interdicted.

In the end it really doesn't matter whether we seize 2 percent, 20 percent, or even 50 percent; no matter how much we seize there will always be enough heroin getting though our barriers to service the addict population. With the relative ease of transporting the drug and the long history of abysmal levels of seizures at the borders, it should be apparent we will never have a truly significant impact on heroin use rate through these kinds of efforts. Logic suggests that the same will hold true for other substances smuggled into the country. Again, it is widely acknowledged that we intercept only a small proportion of drugs that are smuggled into the country, even when we are dealing with bulky items such as marijuana. In 1983 federal officials testifying before a Dade County, Florida, grand jury noted that the United States would have to seize 75 percent of the drugs entering an area before it would be effective in reducing drug use.* Yet we continue to spend a great deal of resources on border-point interdiction, knowing that we can't even approach such a figure. How can this be justified?

The other factor to consider is what would happen to supply if we ignored smuggling. No one knows for sure, as it is not a strategy that has ever been tried, but it is fairly obvious that supplies would increase. That would probably have two effects. For one, the street cost would likely drop and street purity would rise. This is a trend that is already in place and indicates, if nothing else, that recent attempts at interdiction have not been any more successful than past attempts.

---

*Statement contained in speech by Judge Juan Torruella and attributed to Janet Reno, the U.S. Attorney General during the Clinton administration.

The other possible result is more widespread use of heroin in the population. This is not a desirable outcome, but if heroin were still illegal the spread of use would not likely change all that dramatically, even with a ready supply of the drug. After all, in many areas of the world the drug is much more readily available, and the level of use in those populations doesn't change any more significantly than the level of use in the United States.

INTERDICTION AT THE SOURCE

Since we cannot seem to stop drugs at the border, why not stop them at their origin? This is an interdiction strategy that has grown more popular over the past two decades. Some progress has been made in this regard through international cooperation. We have developed programs in the Middle East and Southeast Asia to reduce opium cultivation, and in South America to reduce cocaine cultivation. We have also attempted to eliminate marijuana fields, notably in Mexico. Asa Hutchinson, now former Administrator of the DEA, testifying before a Senate subcommittee in 2002, noted that coca production in Bolivia had been reduced by 70 percent (U.S. Senate, 2002). Interestingly enough, he also suggested that the goal of this strategy is to decrease purity and increase price on the street. It certainly seems like a good idea; if the drug doesn't exist to start with, you don't have to worry about it being smuggled into your country. However, this logic contains a serious flaw when we try to execute it.

According to Goode (1997), the total amount of heroin consumed in the United States (all of it illegal, of course) represents less than 5 percent of the world's raw opium crop. Indeed, the entire world's illicit supply of heroin could be produced in twenty-five to fifty square miles of land. If a person is producing opium legally, he or she might have some large, obvious, cultivated field just outside of town. However, if he or she is growing it illegally, he or she will have a small plot of land, which is probably remote and undetectable by any reasonable surveillance protocol. Of course, even this is unnecessary since skimming off 5 percent of a crop output for illicit use would be fairly easy to accomplish.

Goode goes on to analyze cocaine interdiction. What does it mean if we intercept a ton of cocaine at the border? In the short term, we might find a reduction in purity and an increase in price on the street, but we are unlikely to find a measurable change in the amount on the street. In the medium term, little change will occur because a different smuggler, perhaps using a different route, will simply make up the shortfall. In the long term, nothing will change. This analysis would probably hold even if we were seizing ten or twenty times the amount we currently manage to seize. Then we have the unintended consequences of success.

THE FAILURE OF SUCCESS

As can be seen by the previous analysis, source or border interdiction are doomed strategies if our goal is to eradicate illicit drug usage. Too many economic factors are working against us. That is not to say that there can't be *partial* success from interdiction. Clearly, every milligram of drug seized is one milligram less that is available on the street. That could be enough of a goal in itself. However, ironically, if you start having too much success at interdiction, the final scenario may prove counterproductive.

In 1969 the United States launched "Operation Intercept." The official justification of this initiative was to slow or even stop the flow of drugs across the Mexican/American border. Unofficially, other motives might have been at play. G. Gordon Liddy, of Watergate fame, in his autobiography *Will* claims that the BNDD knew the operation would not really stem the flow of drugs into the United States but also knew it would put great pressure on Mexico, which depended on the border traffic for the economic viability of its northern cities and towns. Operation Intercept involved extensive searches of all vehicular and pedestrian traffic across the border with Mexico. This resulted in long lines and traffic jams while trying to cross the border and, of course, in a serious reduction of tourist traffic. According to Liddy, it was actually an exercise in international extortion. The United States wanted permission to use light aircraft to find marijuana fields and spray them with paraquat. When Mexico declined our suggestion, we launched Operation Intercept not to interdict drugs but to create enough chaos so that Mexico would reconsider, which they did.

Let me interject something about the concept of spraying marijuana fields with paraquat: In the annals of harebrained schemes, this one stands out like a shining star. No one who supported this seems to have considered the likely outcome. Paraquat is an herbicide that operates by stopping energy-producing cells and rapidly desiccating (drying out) the tissue. It takes about forty-eight hours before the leaves start to turn brown and fall off. In the meantime, it is very damaging to human tissue. Ingesting one teaspoon is likely fatal. When added to smoke (as in from marijuana or tobacco), it will destroy the lungs. Now, imagine you were growing marijuana and a small plane flew over and sprayed your crop with something. What would you do? Especially if you had seen this happen before and watched your crop die, it is almost certain you will hasten to harvest what you can before it all dies. If this crop is destined for the American market, the country is going to have a dangerous, quite possibly fatal, new adulterant to deal with. Luckily, the program was never actually carried out.

Operation Intercept was just one example of the attempts of the U.S. government to intercept marijuana coming into the country. A number of other efforts existed, all of which had some level of success. We no doubt do a better job of intercepting marijuana than other illicit drugs because the drug itself is a much higher-volume product and more difficult to smuggle. The end result, though, was the development of domestic hothouse marijuana. People were locally cultivating a form of marijuana called sinsemilla, which had a much higher THC content than the previously imported highest grades. Supplies rose and potency significantly increased. Considering the ease with which marijuana grows, one could make a case for short-sightedness by the government. This really should have been a foreseeable outcome of successful interdiction.

For drugs that are not produced domestically, it may be more difficult to predict the long-term consequences of interdiction. Success has its consequences. If we achieve the goal of increased price of the drug on the street, will that deter people from using the drug, or simply require the users to find an even larger supply of money to buy them? The latter seems as likely as the former. Rather than concentrate on "what ifs," which have no direct measure, let's focus on actual examples from which we can see what really happened. Many more examples of such unintended consequences of interdiction strategies than those presented may exist, and no suggestion is being made that these were really foreseeable. However, considered as a group, they should provide policymakers pause to consider their actions carefully before implementing new measures.

One of the efforts we have made is to attack the production of cocaine in the Peruvian highlands. According to Goode (1997), this attempt led to the rise of the Sendero Luminoso (SL; Shining Path in English), a ruthless terrorist group formed by Abimael Guzman in the 1960s with the avowed aim of instituting a Máoist revolution. One estimate suggests they have been responsible for more than 30,000 deaths. The primary source of funds for their activities appears to have been from the cocaine trade. Choy (2002) suggests the SL received payments from 300,000 coca growers to protect them from the government's crop-eradication program. They also received money for guarding airstrips and ensuring safe passage of the drugs. These people typically attacked farmers rather than protecting them. Thus, an effort to eradicate a source of cocaine allowed the SL to gain a foothold in a region they otherwise probably would not have had much access to and make a handsome profit for their activities. The SL had been on the wane since the mid-1990s, but have recently rebounded by financing themselves through narcotrafficking.

The convoluted nature of the tie-ins in the SL example demonstrates how difficult it would be to predict all of the unintended consequences of an action. For an example that is even more convoluted but is more recent, consider the terrorists attacks on September 11, 2001. Although not very direct, a tie-in with narcotics traffic exists here as well. The organization that was behind those attacks was the Al Qaeda terrorist network, with Osama bin Laden at its head. Bin Laden is originally from Saudi Arabia but at the time of the attacks had headquartered his organization in Afghanistan. The United States helped make the rise to power of the Taliban a reality by covertly backing them against the Soviets. Interestingly enough, even though the Taliban had used profits from narcotics trade to prop up their government and buy arms after throwing the Soviets out of the region, they banned all opium production in July 2000, prescribing the death penalty for violations (Dixon, 2003). At first blush, this seems to be an odd decision. However, one prominent theory is that they were hoarding a large supply of opium and hoping to drive up the price of it on the open market before selling it again. With the fall of the Taliban, production of opium is back up to where it used to be. This is no surprise, when one considers the profits that can be made. One acre of land in wheat production will produce a crop worth $121; that same acre used for opium production will produce a crop worth $5,200. As a result, Afghanistan now produces 75 percent of the world's heroin supply.

According to a story in the January 22, 2004, *Washington Times* by Rowan Scarborough, Al Qaeda's top asset is now heroin production. "In Afghanistan, bin Laden has the benefit of the world's largest poppy crop, as he evades capture in Pakistan's notorious border areas. He is reaping $24 million alone from one narcotics network in Kandahar, Afghanistan." It is unclear if this terrorist group would long survive without access to narcotic profits, but without the ouster of the Soviets from Afghanistan—which eventually led to easy access to the narcotics trade for them—it seems unlikely they would have been or would continue to be as successful in their endeavors as they have been.

In reality, a natural alliance exists between terrorist organizations and illicit drug trafficking. In recent Congressional hearings (U.S. Senate, 2001, 2002) DEA Administrator Asa Hutchinson testified about this connection. In addition to Al Qaeda in Afghanistan and SL in Peru, all of the following have some connection to the illicit drug trade, often directly in sales and smuggling, but also in other aspects such as money laundering: Revolutionary Armed Forces of Colombia (FARC), National Liberation Army—Colombia (ELN), United Wa State Army—Burma (UWSA), Kurdistan Workers Party—Turkey (PKK), and Hizballah in Lebanon. Rand Beers, Assistant Secretary of State for Narcotics and International Law Enforcement Affairs, in the same hearing added in Liberation Tigers of Tamil Eelam—Sri Lanka (LTTE), the triborder Islamic groups that operate in Paraguay at the borders with Argentina and Brazil, which have links to bin Laden, Islamic Movement of Uzbekistan (IMU), Basque Fatherland and Liberty (ETA), and United Self Defense of Colombia (AUC), which is an umbrella organization for many Colombian paramilitary forces. Colombia is now the major supplier of heroin and cocaine to the United States. The country now supplies 75 percent of our heroin and 90 percent of cocaine. It is estimated that FARC and ELN make anywhere from $1 million to $3 million dollars a day in profits from the trade of cocaine and heroin. To emphasize the terrorist aspects of this, FARC has recently simplified the trade: 1 kg of relatively pure cocaine is traded for one AK-47, the latter parachuted in Colombia for pickup in the jungle. Even Irish terrorists were mentioned, although the extent of their activities in illicit drugs is unclear.

In addition to the terrorist connection, plenty of cartels and Mafia-like organizations are involved in the trade. For example, the Herrera family in Durango, Mexico, led to Operation Durango in 1985. Who better to describe the eventual outcome than the government itself? The following is from the National Drug Intelligence Center (NDIC) Web page:

> A major change in the type and quantity of heroin in Chicago took place in 1985 following DEA's Operation Durango, which targeted the Herrera organization's drug operations. The Herrera organization supplied virtually the entire Chicago heroin market with Mexican brown powdered and black tar heroin. The success of Operation Durango limited the availability of Mexican heroin and opened a window of opportunity for Nigerians to smuggle SEA heroin into Chicago. Nigerians had readily available supplies of heroin from sources in Thailand and other areas of Southeast Asia. SEA heroin dominated the Chicago market until the introduction of SA heroin from Colombia in 1992. (National Drug Intelligence Center, 2001)

Thus, shutting down one source successfully resulted in opening up the way for a different source that, if not worse, was certainly no better. Today, South American heroin makes up the majority of heroin sold in this country. It is a much more abundant source than the previous sources and is significantly cheaper.

This same story is repeated for other drugs. For years the Colombian cocaine trade was controlled by Pablo Escobar of the Medellín cartel (see Gray, 1998, for a full account). Escobar apparently rose to power sometime around 1979 or 1980. This group used extremes of violence to maintain their grip. When they murdered presidential candidate Luis Carlos Galan in 1989, they finally invoked what was almost a civil war. The United States joined the effort by sending $65 million in military aid to Bogotá. It is difficult to say if that had any impact, but eventually Escobar plea-bargained himself into a luxury jail built just for him, where he continued business as usual. He "escaped," but was hunted down a year and a half later. When Escobar was killed in 1993 in a hail of police gunfire, it had no real effect on cocaine. Instead, the main trade merely shifted to the Cali cartel. Indeed, while all of this was occurring, the purity and volume on the street in the United States increased and the price dropped.

Still another example of how the law and law enforcement can have unintended consequences revolves around how we treat forms of cocaine. This example was also suggested by Gray (1998). A legal distinction between crack and powdered cocaine HCl exists. Crack is made by mixing cocaine with baking soda to form small "rocks." The name *crack* supposedly derives from the sound the rocks make when heated. This form of cocaine is not effective if snorted, swallowed, or even injected, but it vaporizes below the boiling point of water. One can heat it and inhale the vapors. Inhaling a drug is the most direct route of administration. The drug will hit the brain just seven seconds afterward. The result is that any addictive drug, whatever it is, becomes far more seductive. As a result, it takes less total drug usage (and less money) to really hook someone, and cocaine is a very seductive drug to begin with.

Because of its potential for damage, laws at both the state and federal level require a harsher penalty for the possession or sale of crack than for powdered cocaine. Few would argue that this distinction should not be made because it is inherent in the nature of delivery that crack is a worse problem than snorting the powdered form. But then you look one step further, we discover that people who are better off financially are not buying their cocaine on the street corner; they buy it in more protected places and are more likely to buy powder than crack. Crack users are disproportionately at the bottom of the financial ladder and are disproportionately black and Hispanic. According to Gray (1998), although the "vast majority" of people who have used crack are white, 96 percent of crack defendants in federal courts are black or Hispanic. The end result of this distinction is that the disenfranchised most often pay the penalty for the use of this drug. Surely no one intended to produce legislation that would be racist in application, but that was the eventual outcome.

THE FAILURE OF SUCCESS II: INTENDED CONSEQUENCES

Sometimes intended consequences can be just as much of a disaster as unintended ones, although you typically will still have people arguing the outcome is a good thing. Consider the price of drugs on the street. One of the stated goals of the drug laws is to drive the price up so fewer people will use them. It probably is true that fewer will start to use an expensive drug compared to a drug that is cheap, but those who are already doing it, or those who start using despite the cost, now have the problem of feeding an even more expensive habit. What do they do? If they are typical they will probably use illegal activities of one form or another to supply themselves. In turn, that high cost just feeds even more money into the coffers of the drug dealers, improving their already outrageous profit margin and further ensuring that they stay in business.

If we want an example of how this works all we need to do is consider alcohol. The actual production cost of alcohol is dirt cheap. When I was in graduate school in the 1970s we were conducting research on alcoholism using pigtailed monkeys as subjects. One day I had to get a gallon of 190-proof alcohol from a university-maintained warehouse. I don't have a clear memory of the exact cost, but it was around $1. It was that cheap because no profit or taxes were involved in the sale. Even back then, alcohol in a liquor store probably would have cost $50 to $100 for that much. So why isn't there a huge black market for alcohol? Because a legal supply exists, and that legal supply, even with all the taxes and profit margins for sellers, is still well within most people's means. In terms of recreational drugs, alcohol remains among the cheapest of them. In other words, the cost simply is not high enough to make it worthwhile for people to seek out and buy moonshine in preference to the legal varieties.

However, what happened to alcohol as a result of prohibition? Alcohol consumption declined dramatically following passage of the law (although it had already been on a downward trend), but then started to rebound and gradually increased through the mid-1920s until its repeal. Then the cost of a drink rose dramatically (Thornton, 1991). The cost of beer (probably because of its relative bulk) rose 700 percent, brandy 433 percent, and distilled spirits 270 percent. This had the effect of shifting drinking allegiance away from beer and wine toward "hard liquor," due both to price and bulk issues when using illicit drugs. The real issue, however, is not so much price, or what people chose to drink; the most important issue is that this is how organized crime got its first real foothold on widespread drug distribution. As intended, fewer people drank, but more so because of the fact

that it was illegal than because it was expensive. With the end of prohibition and the subsequent drop in prices of drinks (besides allowing
it to be served openly again), organized crime was largely taken out of
the alcohol distribution equation, although it still continued as part of
legitimate business. On balance, most people seem to feel that alcohol prohibition, even though it met its intended goals, caused more
damage than good. If alcohol were made illegal again, it is probable
that the price of a drink would rise and plenty of black market activity
would surface to supply consumers either with foreign alcohol or
moonshine.

Can we apply that analogy to illicit drugs such as heroin or cocaine? Probably not, because even though some will argue for legalization of these drugs, realistically it is not going to happen. But what
about policies that allow the price of drugs on the street to drop? No
doubt more people *would* use them if they were cheaper and readily
available, but a savings would appear in other areas, such as crime
committed to support drug habits. Right now, due to enforcement efforts, the price of illicit drugs on the street is artificially high (compared to what it would be if they were legal). So where is the balance
point? Is it better or worse that we keep the price of drugs artificially
inflated? The answer to that will depend on your own value system
and where you place your priorities. Reasonable people will be found
on each side of this issue.

Finally, another assumption must be challenged: the concept that if
the price goes high enough, people will use less (that is, that use levels are price-sensitive). This is surely true for commodities in general—even necessary ones. If the price of gasoline goes up, even
though people need to use gasoline, the overall use rate will eventually drop as people try to conserve. Certainly, if the price were to
drop, the result would be even more use. Yet, paradoxically perhaps,
that just doesn't seem to happen with drugs. Heroin use has remained
relatively stable since 1988 despite drastic drops in prices. The correlation (r) between the price of heroin and the total amount used in this
country is very low ($r = +0.121$) (ONDCP, 2001b). With the number
of data points used, that number does not differ significantly from
zero. In other words, no relationship between how much heroin costs
and how much is used can be found. Addict use levels are driven by
need and desire, and remain relatively immune to prices. The stated

goal of reducing heroin use by increasing the street price, then, is chasing a fantasy.

In contrast to this, cocaine use is *not* unrelated to price, but the results in this case are distinctly counterintuitive and can only be described as remarkable. The level of cocaine use in the United States has been steadily dropping for some time, probably because it is being replaced with methamphetamine use. A correlation between the price of cocaine and the total amount used produces a strong positive relationship ($r = +0.777$)! In other words, as the price of cocaine was falling rapidly, so was the level of use. If we were to naively apply the reasoning that price could be used to control drug-use levels, then the idiotic conclusion we would reach is that we should increase the availability on the street in order to get people to use less.

INTERDICTION AT THE USER LEVEL

User-level sales, from a pusher to the actual user, can take place two ways. One way is behind closed doors between a buyer and the pusher. The other is on the street. In the former, it is more likely that the two parties have an established pattern of repeated sales between them. With the latter, that is less likely; rather than people it's the location that is the key element in making the connection. Attempting to interdict these sales will therefore require two kinds of strategies.

At this point, the federal government won't be spending most of the money. This is primarily a job for local police with some help from state and federal agencies. However, it is still part of the same concept for fighting the war on drugs. The level of interdiction obtained will be functions of both time and locale. For instance, depending on where you are (that is, in which city or town you live) and the amount of resources remain available in the annual budget for law enforcement, you will get greater or lesser efforts. Presumably, the more time, resources, and effort, the greater the level of success. The same economic factors that work against you at the larger, international scale are present at the local level. Because the profits to be made in selling illicit drugs are so outrageous, a shortage of people selling will never occur, no matter what the risks.

Let's start by examining the price of heroin on the street in New York City, which traditionally has had some of the lowest prices. At

the very beginning, heroin was very cheap. Malichi Harney (superin-
tendent, Division of Narcotic Control, Illinois) in 1958 noted that in
1920, heroin was selling for $12 to $20 per ounce. With just over
twenty-eight grams to the ounce, that would be only forty-two cents
to seventy-one cents per gram, although purity wasn't specified. Ad-
justing for inflation, that would be $3.89 to $6.57 today. By the mid-
1930s the price had risen to a range of $38.12 to $47.72 and by 1958 it
was $113 to $226, all numbers adjusted for inflation to today's values. The price continued to rise until the period between 1990 and
1992, but since then the price of heroin has been dropping and the purity increasing. This trend is mirrored around the country, but the exact figures vary from location to location. It is not completely uniform, with some years showing a reversal of the overall trend, which
is no doubt based on multiple factors. However, New York City has
always been a bastion of narcotic sales, so it seems to be a good place
to start. Thirty-five years ago an addict would probably make a buy
that ranged from 3 percent to as high as 6 to 7 percent pure; in 2000,
purity in New York City on the street ranged from 30 to 80 percent.
Thirty-five years ago, a gram of pure heroin cost about $500
(Brecher, 1972, pp. 91-93); in 2000, according to the NDIC Web page
(November 2000), one gram of pure heroin cost about $140 on aver-
age ($65 to $70 per gram at 50 percent purity). Factor in inflationary
pressures on the dollar over a thirty-five-year time span, and the drop
in cost is stunning. That $500 in 1972 would be the equivalent of
$2,125 in 2000 (using Federal Reserve calculations at <http://www.
minneapolisfed.org/Research/data/us/calc/>). Hence, the cost of heroin dropped to less than 7 percent of what it was only thirty years before. Brecher also reports the cost of Turkish black market heroin at
its source to be only $25 per kg in 1971, giving a total markup of the
drug at 2000 percent. Most of this drop in price, coupled with increased purity on the street, has appeared since 1990; it seems to be
correlated with the development of South American (SA) heroin as a
source.

Another recent trend is for fewer middlemen to be involved in the
pipeline, so our hypothetical pusher may be only one or two steps removed from the importer. In Chicago, for example, it depends on
whether one is going through the Mexican or Nigerian connection.
With or without a middleman, the drug is passed on to gangs, which then
vend on the street. These gang members are typically young—either

teenagers or early twenties—and are usually considered expendable. To limit the losses in case someone gets arrested they normally are given only eleven packets. Most of the packets are "dime bags," small pieces of aluminum foil folded around the product, which they will sell for $10 each. The pusher pays the source for ten of them and the profit they receive is in the eleventh, which they can either sell or keep for personal use.

No matter how many people are involved, though, the basic technique is the same. The product is "cut" by adding some other substance, which results in lower purity; then the adulterated product is sold at the same or higher price as the original. The importer is selling heroin at $70 to $90 per gram, typically 85 to 90 percent pure. By the time it gets to the street, it is still the same price, but the purity may be only 50 percent. Hence, the product has almost doubled in cost and the difference is virtually pure profit. If the importer is selling for $78 per pure gram, the addict is buying at $140 per pure gram, and the costs of the adulterant are negligible, then someone is making a profit of more than $60 per gram. This is true for every gram sold. Since the addict requires a daily set amount for his habit, then he or she must make a buy on a very regular basis. Looking at the averages among New York, Chicago, and San Diego, based on a 1994 study, the average an addict will spend is $47.36 a day, which translates into just under 75 mg of pure drug. This results in a $17,238-a-year habit, and roughly $7,400 in profit per year per client for the pipeline after the drug makes it through the border. For a comparison, imagine you ran a business that provided clients a particular service. You need only spend a few minutes with each client, and you have more clients than you can really handle. If you can service just thirty clients a day you will make a net profit of $222,000 per year. The best thing is that they want your service so much they will seek you out to get it.

The actual price per milligram on the street varies dramatically across the country. This is partly due to differences in origin of supply, which, in turn, is partly due to primary port of entry. The three largest import areas are New York, Chicago, and Los Angeles. The four primary points of origin are Southeast Asia (SEA), Mexico (MEX), Southwest Asia (SWA), and South America (SA). The SA connection is beginning to dominate the United States markets primarily because it is much cheaper. SA-sourced heroin also tends to be of higher purity when it hits the streets. DEA official sources for selected cities in 2001 include the following:

City	Average purity	Average price/mg pure
New York	57%	$0.98
Chicago	20%	$0.67
Philadelphia	73%	$0.40
Baltimore	27%	$0.32
Los Angeles	16%	$1.00
San Francisco	10%	$1.87
San Diego	45%	$0.26

These examples were chosen to show a middle range of values. A more complete listing can be found in Appendix III. An interesting side note to this list is that Baltimore is now reported to have the highest rate of heroin addiction in the United States, at 58.5 per 1,000 residents (according to a statement by DEA Administrator Thomas Constantine before a House Committee hearing on June 16, 1999).

Several things must be noted about these data. One is that the average price per mg varies not only by locality but by year in sometimes dramatic fashion. For example, in Houston, from 1997 through 2001, the price per mg of pure heroin was $2.20, $2.43, $1.16, $1.04, and $1.53, respectively. The difference from low to high was more than 200 percent and, in one year, a 209 percent drop in price occurred.

The other interesting factor to note is the inverse relationship between price and purity. Overall, across the nation, if we correlate purity and price on the street, we obtain a correlation coefficient of –0.52. In other words, as the purity goes up, the price per mg of the pure drug tends to drop. This would seem to indicate that the same factors that allow purity to increase drive the price down, and availability is the most likely source effect. When the supply is firm, the street quality rises and the price drops. This gets more interesting when you divide the country along the Mississippi River. In the eastern half of the United States, it's a relatively small inverse relationship, with $r = -0.16$. But in the western half of the nation it's a very strong effect, with $r = -0.72$. If St. Louis, which has an anomalously high price for heroin, is removed, the correlation coefficient becomes an astounding –0.94 between the purity of the drug on the street and the price per pure mg. (If you add St. Louis to the eastern states, that –0.16 becomes –0.44.) It is unclear why this should occur, other than the fact that the western half of the nation appears to be dominated by Mexican heroin while the eastern half has been taken over by South American heroin.

This relationship between price and availability would probably be fuel for those people determined to eliminate the drug. They would suggest, no doubt, that the drop in price on the street would result in both more users and higher use levels per person. However, another side must be considered. Most hard-core heroin addicts must support their habits with crime. With the drop in price on the street they would presumably have to commit fewer crimes. Again, this is not a zero-sum game; losing on one front in the battle against drugs might actually have a net positive effect when other factors are taken into consideration. It should also be noted that the radical drop in price and rise in quality is yet another indication that interdiction simply isn't working well.

Street-level interdiction requires the presence of officers of enforcement. Since it is readily apparent that we are unable to clog the pipeline of drugs to the street, this is the last bastion of interdiction. It should be axiomatic that we could interdict street-level sales—at least those that take place in public—by greatly increasing the levels of law enforcement. However, this concept has an obvious limitation. How many police officers would it take? Remarkably, fully interdicting sales on the street has actually been done at least twice.

The following information was published in the op-ed section of the *Orange County Register,* on September 10, 1996 (reproduced from <http://www.vcl.org/Judges/VBrown_Mag.htm>). It is based on an account by Volney Brown, former U.S. Magistrate, about operations he oversaw in Phoenix and San Diego under the Office of Drug Abuse Law Enforcement (ODALE).

Initially, using a very large pot of "buy money," ODALE bought from every street dealer they could find and determined that seventy-six drug pushers were in Phoenix at that time. With assistance from the state and local police, all seventy-six were arrested at one time. Brown states:

> For a week it was impossible to buy drugs on the streets of Phoenix. The single local drug treatment program was swamped. Addicts who could not get treatment left town to score elsewhere. But on the eighth day, new street pushers began to appear in the

city, and before a month had elapsed, it was business-as-usual. We had spent tens of thousands of federal tax dollars, and sent scores of pushers to prison, but there was no lasting effect on the availability or price of illicit drugs.

Essentially the same program was tried again in San Diego. They determined that almost all of the heroin being sold there was being sold by a local gang. Using wiretaps, which the state and local police could not use due to California law, and "thousands of employee hours," they obtained enough evidence and, like Phoenix, arrested everyone in one night. But the story written in Phoenix was repeated in San Diego. Despite making it almost impossible to buy heroin on the street for a week, it started to reappear after eight days, and within a month it was impossible to see any change in the heroin traffic. Quoting Brown again:

> We had spent hundreds of thousands of federal tax dollars, and we sent every one of the 39 pushers to federal prison, but there was no lasting effect on the availability of heroin or its price. In one respect we were worse off for our success. Before, we knew who was selling, but afterwards we had no idea . . .
> But in the end, in our territory it was not more difficult or more expensive to obtain illegal drugs than it was in the beginning. We had failed to solve, or even affect, the "drug problem" with law enforcement. If we had been given 10 or 20 times the resources, we still would have failed.

Here is an account of someone who spent time in the trenches, attempting to interdict heroin trafficking at the street level. He was successful in his battles but ultimately made little impact in the war. Starting with a much larger budget than would be available to a city and employing law enforcement techniques prohibited by state law, ODALE was able to secure the short-term goal of eliminating heroin traffic in a relatively local area. Then they make the astonishing admission that they could not accomplish their goals long term *even with up to twenty times their already large budget!* Brown remained proud of the efforts of ODALE and continued to look upon these results as victories even if they provided only a ripple in the fabric of drug sales. After all, for a short period of time, heroin was denied to addicts and people who were profiting from that trade were punished.

However, the long-term impact of these benefits was so slight that it hardly seems worth the effort.

What can be learned from this? Even if an entire city budget were spent on nothing but providing police officers on the street, it would not be enough. No matter how attractive it seems to hammer the people who are selling the drug, if our goal is to reduce or eliminate drug use, it is the wrong strategy to employ. Other strategies are likely to have greater success and are significantly cheaper than interdiction efforts. We will address these in subsequent Chapters 6 and 7.

INTERDICTION FOR COCAINE
AND CRACK COCAINE

The story for cocaine is even more dramatic than that for heroin. The profits available from the sale of cocaine on the street are staggering. Unlike heroin, cocaine addicts will vary their use depending largely on personal economic factors. A heroin user, while progressive, will not typically use much higher doses even if they are available, nor will they use less simply because they run short of money. Cocaine is horribly seductive, but if an addict runs out of money he or she can put off taking it without suffering withdrawal. Conversely, if one happens to make a big score one is likely to use much more than usual until it is gone. For the seller, though, it is always a ready market with plenty of buyers, regardless of price.

What kind of profits are we talking about here? Gray (1998) begins his book with the story of Chicago Police Detective Frank Goff and the arrest of De-De, a delivery man for the Gangster Disciples. When caught, De-De had $53,000 in cash and 7.7 kg of powdered cocaine. At today's prices, that would be worth about $962,000 on the street—nearly 1 million dollars in cash and product. How much of this represented his own personal profit is not clear, but it seems likely that he was making enough money to have a "comfortable" life. Receipts he had indicated he had collected $451,000 in the first ten days of March 1995. The Gangster Disciples were taking a 300 percent markup in drug price. Thus, those receipts indicate a ten-day profit of $300,000 for the gang! De-De, of course, was not the only seller of cocaine for the gang. The figures are more than staggering—they are mind bending.

Where else can a group of largely uneducated people reap an annual profit of $11 million per salesman?

By 1988, crack had become the most frequently sold and most lucrative drug in the street drug market (Johnson, Golub, and Fagan, 1995). Substantial proportions of heroin users, cocaine snorters, and marijuana users reported having sold crack and having earned higher incomes from its sale than from their sales of other drugs or from the commission of nondrug crimes. Although many crack users also reported other drug use, they reported much more crack use than anything else. This was even true for half of the heroin users who used both drugs.

As with heroin, an inverse relationship exists between the purity of powder cocaine on the street and its price, with a correlation coefficient of $r = -0.48$. However, in contrast to heroin, price and purity of cocaine do not vary as much among regions. The average price is $83 per gram and the average purity is 61 percent. New York is anomalously cheap at $29 per gram, which lowers the average price. More statistics can be found in Appendix IV. A better number to use might be the median, which is $90 per gram. It is much more difficult to get a reliable estimate of the price of crack cocaine. The average price per gram is a little higher than the powdered form at $96 per gram, but the range is much greater and the purity is typically not reported. Nevertheless, it is likely a more profitable venture than selling heroin. If the economics of heroin suggest it's a trade that is impossible to shut down, then the analysis holds even more so for cocaine.

MARIJUANA INTERDICTION

Preventing the traffic in marijuana is simultaneously easier and even more impossible than interdicting cocaine or heroin. It is easier because it is so much bulkier and, therefore, more difficult to transport or hide in equal dollar amounts than are the other drugs. However, it is also more difficult because it is so ubiquitous. It is by far the most widely used illicit drug, and this use cuts across all strata of society. According to the National Survey on Drug Use and Health, of the 14.6 million past-month marijuana users in 2002, about one-third, or 4.8 million persons, used it on twenty or more days in the past month. As many as 40 percent of Americans have used marijuana or hashish at least once in their lifetimes—even some relatively well-known politicians (although at least one claims not to have inhaled). Trends in new users have held fairly steady over the past decade, as have levels of lifetime use. This implies that not much has changed recently in the level of marijuana use.

Unlike heroin or cocaine, the raw product of marijuana does not have to be smuggled across the border. It is grown clandestinely all through the United States in hothouses and remote fields. Domestic production is still less than the demand, and this situation is likely to remain for some time. Thus, huge profits can still be made from smuggled marijuana, which means large quantities are still brought in from other countries.

FINAL COSTS OF INTERDICTION

Resources are limited. We do not have an unlimited pot of money to draw upon for law enforcement. At some point, we must prioritize what money we have to spend and make decisions about on what we should spend it. If we shift too much effort into the war on drugs, we are likely to suffer unwanted consequences in other areas. Baum (1993) stated:

> The shibboleth that increased drug enforcement can reduce other types of crime is questioned by studies in Florida and Chicago, where diverting extensive police resources to drug enforcement had the unintended consequence of allowing both property crime and alcohol-related traffic deaths to increase. (p. 71)

What do we actually spend? In the ONDCP budget summary published on September 1, 2001, the final total amount spent across nineteen U.S. divisions housed in six U.S. agencies in 1999 to reduce the supply of drugs was $5,867,500,000 (found at <http://www.whitehousedrugpolicy.gov/publications/pdf/economic_costs98.pdf>, Table B-12). If all aspects of federal spending on eliminating illicit drugs were added together, the figure would be much higher. Ten years ago, according to Judge Juan Toruella in the ONDCP budget summary, we were already spending $12.1 billion for drug enforcement at the federal level. It is unclear if some of this money might be encumbered regardless of whether we were attempting to interdict drugs, but this is the official number generated by the government itself. It includes more than $1.3 billion for the DEA and more than $1 billion for the Department of Defense. It does not reflect money spent at the state or local level. The same publication estimates the total crime-related costs to the nation of drug abuse in 1999 at more than $97 billion and total societal costs of drugs at $143 billion in 1998.

If illicit drugs came from only one source and no realistic alternatives existed, or if all illicit drugs came through one port of entry or one organization, it might be possible to prevent them. However, illicit drugs come to us through organizations that have a great deal of money to spend, and the market has plenty of competition if one source gets shut down. The goal of this chapter was to demonstrate that it is impossible to successfully interdict illicit drugs at *any* level. No matter how much of our resources we put into it, interdiction is simply not going to have any long-term, measurable effect. If we really want to fight a war on drugs, this is the wrong battleground to choose.

Chapter 5

Failures of Incarceration

A possible subtitle for this chapter might be "Why Prison Won't Work." We have tried harsh penalties to little avail, and we have thrown a lot of money at the problem in an attempt to lock up drug criminals without solving the problem. In other words, we have a history of this type of strategy not working. The truth is that it's a strategy that is mostly doomed to failure no matter how harsh the penalties or how many police officers we have to enforce the laws. That may sound surprising; if it does, it is because you aren't a criminal. Let's start by examining the state of the criminal justice system as it now exists.

CURRENT STATE OF PRISONS

Baum (1993) reported that we spend twice as much money on law enforcement as we do on treatment and education. Depending on accounting practices and definitions, this might have changed in the past decade, but it still remains the main repository of money and efforts. The end result of treating illicit drugs as primarily a criminal problem rather than focusing on prevention and treatment is that, according to the Walmsley (2004) report of 205 countries, the United States has become the nation with the largest percentage of its people behind bars, with 701 out of 100,000 people in jail or prison (http://www.homeoffice.gov.uk/rds/pdfs2/r234.pdf). Between 1980 and 1993, the United States doubled the number of people in prison. Nearly all of this increase was due to illicit drug violations, either possession or sale, and much of the increase results from mandatory sentencing guidelines (see Chapter 3). By 1999, 62 percent of federal prisoners convicted of a drug-related crime had mandatory sentences, more than half of them for an excess of five years (Scalia, 2001).

Some of this is also due to increased levels of law enforcement, although whether that indicates increased effectiveness is unclear. In November 2003, the Federal Bureau of Prisons listed official numbers of persons in federal prisons from 1970 to 2002, and broke this down by proportion of prisoners who were convicted of drug-related offenses. This would exclude someone who might have committed a federal crime, such as bank robbery, to get money to buy drugs unless they were arrested specifically for possession or sale of drugs. According to Mumola (1999), 16 percent of federal inmates, 19 percent of state inmates, and 18 percent of convicted jail inmates reported they committed their crime to obtain money to buy drugs. That is, not all drug-related crime is included in these figures. By 1993, the number of people in federal prison for drug violations was greater than the entire federal prison population of 1980. By 2003, the number of people in federal prison for drug violations was greater than the entire federal prison population of 1993. The full table is presented in Appendix V.

Between 1973 and 1983, the numbers were fairly stable in terms of both total prison population and the proportion that was in for drug offenses. Over that time period, the average sentenced population of prisoners (excluding those waiting for final disposition) was 22,182 and the average proportion of those in for drug offenses was 26.3 percent. Then the situation began to change. Gradually, over the next few years, the number of federal prisoners rose, as did the proportion of drug offenders. Between 1985 and 1992, the proportion changed an average of 3.75 percent per year, while the overall numbers grew at an average of about 4,000 prisoners per year. The proportion peaked in 1994 at 61.3 percent, held steady for a few years, and then gradually subsided to 54.7 percent in 2003. However, the numbers grew alarmingly from 1992 to 2003, increasing from 59,516 inmates to 128,090. Because the proportion of drug crimes dropped slightly, it is clear that an influx of all kinds of federally prosecuted crimes has occurred, but drug-related offenses still make up the majority of these; without them, the number of other federal offenses would probably decrease as well.

This is all very costly. It takes a good deal of money to run a prison system. You have to build the prisons, maintain them in some semblance of working order, and hire staff to guard and manage the prisoners. You must also feed and clothe the prisoners, and look after their health needs. Other mandated costs can include maintaining a prison law library, drug rehabilitation programs, or educational programs. The actual cost is very difficult to estimate, as all of these figures will change with the level of security needed and the geographic location. Remember that this is only the end of the prisoner pipeline—it also costs money to prosecute people and to keep tabs on prisoners when they are released.

The actual costs per year for a prisoner in the federal system as it now stands depends on your source, which, in turn, depends on the assumptions being made. For example, one fairly low estimate that combines state and federal prisons is $20,236 per prisoner (http://www.mpp.org/arrests/fas61699.html). In contrast, in testimony before a July 13, 1999, Congressional hearing, Kings County, New York, District Attorney Charles Hynes suggested it costs $30,000 per prisoner per year. As part of a legal proceeding *(United States v. Hively)*, Judge Myron Bright of the 8th Circuit Court of Appeals reported the 1994 cost of a prisoner in the federal system was $21,352 per year.* Adjusted for inflation, that would be $26,481 in 2003. Thus, using this intermediate figure, with approximately 73,000 people incarcerated in federal prison in 2003 for drug offenses, the total cost is about $1,933,100,000. With all the assumptions and averaging that has to be done to achieve these numbers, we might as well just round in off to $2 billion. It should not be surprising, then, that the Bush administration restructured budget categories to remove the costs of housing prisoners from the budgetary costs of the war on drugs; this new accounting practice allows the government to report a higher percentage of the money budgeted to fight the war on drugs as being spent on education and treatment. This change is merely cosmetic, since the money is going to be spent anyway—it is just how the government accounts for it.

This bears some emphasis. We spend almost $2 billion per year just to *house* drug offenders, and that fact does not change whether it is charged to the war on drugs or to something else. Now for "the rest of the story." We still aren't done with the legal costs. The judicial and legal costs of prosecuting alleged felons, not counting the costs of catching them in the first place, averages around $17,100 each. This

---

*Letter from Kathleen M. Hawk, Director, U.S. Department of Justice, Federal Bureau of Prisons, to the Honorable Myron H. Bright (July 6, 1995). *United States v. Hiveley,* 61 F.3d 1358 at 1363.

number reflects the prorated costs of maintaining a court system, salaries for court officials, and costs of trials (as well as costs of plea-bargained agreements which are vastly cheaper). That raises the total prison bill to more than $3 billion per year for the judiciary and Federal Bureau of Prisons to handle drug offenses. Now add in $34,867 per inmate on average for the required police and other law enforcement personnel (obtained from <http://www.drugwarfacts.org/prison.htm>, pp. 4-5) and we easily pay more than $5.5 billion per year to deal with drug offenders in the legal pipeline. These numbers are current for 2002 and should be a close estimate for today's actual cost (about $5.87 billion in 2005).

What if we need to build more prisons? Two relatively new prisons are located in Hazelton, West Virginia, and Inez, Kentucky. They are each designed to house between 900 and 1,000 prisoners. The costs of construction are estimated at $137 million and $146 million, respectively. In general, the cost of a new prison will range from $50,000 to $200,000 per prisoner housed (Torruella, 1996). This cost will eventually have to be considered as part of the war on drugs as well. After all, without the huge influx of drug offenders, all of our prisons would have more empty space instead of being chronically overcrowded.

If things continue as they are now, we are going to need to construct new prisons even without continuing the war on drugs or start turning prisoners loose before they have completed their mandatory sentences. All our prison systems are strained to the limits. Department of Justice numbers indicate that state prisons around the country are running from 1 percent to 16 percent over rated capacity, while the federal system is at 33 percent over capacity (obtained from <http://www.ojp.usdoj.gov/bjs/abstract/p02.htm>). This is a heritage of our culture: either we have more crime and criminals in this country than the rest of the world does or we prosecute and imprison lawbreakers at a higher rate. It is astonishing that the United States has the highest rate in the world of incarcerating people at 686 per 100,000 (Walmsley, 2003). This number includes those in prison serving sentences and those waiting trial. In contrast, the United Kingdom has a rate of 139 per 100,000. This is the highest rate in the European Union, and is still above the midpoint of the world, but is only 20 percent as high as that of the United States. Canada's rate is even lower at 102 per 100,000, around 15 percent as high as that of the United States. Some of this is driven by cultural considerations that have nothing to do with drugs, but drug-related offenses remain the largest part of the federal prison population and a significant part of jail and state prison populations.

Yet even this isn't the full story. When we add those on probation or parole to the incarcerated population we reach the astounding figure of 6,732,400 adults in the prison pipeline by the end of 2002 (obtained from <http://www.ojp.usdoj.gov/bjs/pub/press/ppus02pr.htm>). That's 3.1 percent of the adult population of the nation.

CURRENT STATE OF THE COURTS

Samuel Walker (1985, pp. 33-35) proposed a theory he called "the law of criminal justice thermodynamics." The concept is partly based on there being some physical limitations on the court system. With unlimited resources available, the police and courts could handle any size caseload. Of course, the reality is that the courts are already overcrowded, with some cases waiting excessive periods of time before working their way through the system. The theory is that the system will respond to such pressures by finding some way to regulate its workload. For instance, if severe penalties are mandated, the system will find a way to apply those penalties less frequently, often by bargaining down to lesser crimes. This analysis is somewhat moot today once the suspect has been arrested, due to the new mandatory sentencing guidelines, but it doesn't have to be the court or prosecutor making the adjustment. Walker reports that the effect of a Massachusetts law mandating a one-year term for carrying a firearm resulted in the police conducting fewer frisks. If you don't look for a firearm, then you don't have to arrest as many people for that crime.

A classic case of this principle in action took place in New York State. The State passed new laws that took effect in 1973 that made it the toughest state in the nation on drug crimes. Analyzing what happened in New York between 1972 and 1976, Walker (1985, pp. 67-71) noted that adjustments on administration of the law made the effects of these new laws moot even if certain people did feel the brunt of these laws. Although some people bore much harsher penalties after 1973, it was also true that fewer people reached that point. The proportion of arrests that led to indictments dropped between 1972 and

1976, as did the percentage of indictments that led to convictions. In 1972, 34 percent of arrests resulted in convictions; by 1976 that had dropped to 20 percent. On the other hand, a higher percentage of convicted persons went to prison in 1976, and the terms on average were longer; in particular, this was true for those receiving a sentence of three years or more. The end result of all of the adjustments was that in 1972, 11 percent of persons arrested for drug possession or sale went to prison. In 1976, 11 percent of persons arrested for drug possession or sale went to prison, although on average for a longer stay. In the meantime, an additional cost surfaced: The number of arrested persons demanding actual trials rose from 6 percent in 1972 to 15 percent in 1976, and trials are vastly more expensive in both dollars and man-hours than plea bargains or non-tried cases.

All of these adjustments would have been irrelevant if the new laws worked. If passing new, harsh laws actually reduced the use of drugs almost everyone would feel the extra time and money would be well spent and no one would worry very much about internal adjustments made by the system. Unfortunately, as with the rest of the country, actual drug use in New York rose during that time period. It seems highly unlikely the new laws *caused* the rise in drug use, but equally clear the new laws did not work the way they were intended to. Indeed, even the justice department concluded it was impossible to substantiate the popular claim that mandatory sentencing reduces crime (Walker, 1985, p. 67). With the failure to achieve its goals manifest, New York backed off and repealed many of the new provisions in 1979.

In the decade from 1980 to 1990 the number of drug cases brought before federal courts tripled, while the number of sitting judges declined (Baum, 1993). This clogged up the court system even more, making it even more difficult for judges to finish a calendar. No doubt the law of criminal justice thermodynamics continues to work, but how far we can push such adjustments is limited. And as noted in Chapter 2, the adjustments are now taking place at the level of the prosecutor's office rather than at trial.

THE CRIMINAL MIND-SET

Why don't harsh penalties work? Consider this proposition: Think of an activity that you enjoy. If possible, make it a drug-related activity. Perhaps it is drinking coffee or tea, smoking a cigarette, or drinking homemade wine, or maybe it is jogging on the sidewalk before going to work. Imagine the government declares that activity illegal. What will you do? For me, the example would be coffee. I love my coffee—strong, fresh-brewed, caffeine-laced coffee. Suppose some study finds caffeine to be carcinogenic and it is declared illegal. Will I risk going to jail or paying a fine to continue to enjoy my morning coffee? I think not. I might be angry, write letters to my congressman, organize political protests, write letters to the editor, march in protest at the Capitol with like-minded people—any number of activities. But risk going to jail, or paying even a modest fine, such as $100? The threat of jail, even if not highly likely, would be plenty to deter me. How about you? What activity do you enjoy so much that you would be willing to risk jail time to continue doing it? The list is probably a short one.

That is because you are a law-abiding citizen. It may seem counterintuitive, but just making an activity illegal, even with very modest penalties, will produce close to the same level of overall compliance as attaching draconian penalties to that behavior *for the average law-abiding citizen*. Furthermore, the people who write the laws are similar to you and me in that regard. That is the citizen mind-set. The difficult thing to comprehend is that criminals operate from an entirely different mind-set.

I had the opportunity to teach classes from time to time at Oxford Federal Correctional Institution, a medium- to high-level security prison located in central Wisconsin, as part of a program that allowed prisoners to earn college degrees. It was an interesting experience, to say the least, and it allowed me to gain some insight into the differences between them as a group of people and the rest of society. Here is part of a conversation I had with a prisoner the very first time I taught there:

The prisoner/student was a very personable man, pleasant in demeanor and easy to talk to. He had been arrested for bank robbery. Prior to the war on drugs, that was probably the most common crime that landed people in the federal prison system. At the level of prison Oxford was, people didn't get sent there for a first offense unless special circumstances were involved. This was the student's sixth time in prison; each time had been for bank robbery. So I asked him: "You robbed banks and were caught and sent to prison five times before.

Why did you do it a sixth time?" His answer was quite instructive. He said, in a very casual, offhanded manner, "I thought I had figured out what I was doing wrong." He wasn't the least deterred by being in prison. It was abundantly clear that he felt no remorse about committing a crime, only at not being smart enough to get away with it. I have no doubt that if he now thought he had it figured out, as soon as he was released he was going to try it again. As far as deterrence goes, if the sentence next time was a mandatory twenty years instead of three to five (or whatever the penalty was at that time), it would not have made the least bit of difference to him. What mattered was not the penalty for getting caught but whether he believed that he could get away with it.

Abundant evidence shows that harsh penalties do not actually do much to deter crime. This is a difficult concept to believe, because we know in our hearts that it sure would deter us. However, we aren't the criminals we are trying to deter. Goode (1993, p. 127) notes several generalizations about criminals. Among them are that the persons who commit the most serious crimes also commit less serious ones (although the reverse does not hold true), that the arrest ratio for crimes actually committed runs only about 0.4 to 0.6 percent, and that the more serious the individual's criminal involvement, the less likely that incarcerations will act as a deterrent to crime. Even a 1994 Department of Justice analysis noted boldly that recidivism rates for nonviolent drug offenders are unaffected by the amount of time spent in prison, whether recidivism is measured by parole revocation, rearrest, reconviction, or return to prison.

Kurt Schmoke (1988), former mayor of Baltimore, noted three factors about drug dealers that, taken together, explain why this is. First, going to jail is considered part of the cost of doing business. The profits in the drug trade are so high that paying for criminal acts with a prison term is part of the price that they figure into their personal equations up front. Second, drug criminals fear one another far more than they fear the police; the police have to give them due process, but other dealers will simply kill them. Third, where else can they make this much money? If the competitive business practices of their rivals (murder, extortion, and kidnapping) fail to deter the drug trafficker, what chance does a long jail term have? It would take prison terms of such lengths or other punishments insupportable in a democracy to have much of an impact on the typical drug dealer.

PROBLEMS WITH MANDATORY
SENTENCING GUIDELINES

Setting and enforcing harsh penalties in an effort to deter crime, then, does not seem to work very well. Mandatory minimum sentences do nothing to change this equation. As Tonrey (1992) noted, mandatory sentencing not only has little effect, but as an instrument of public policy it does more harm than good. Unrelated to harshness of the law in general, mandatory sentencing guidelines produce several other problems.

The way the law reads, the weight of the drug is added to the weight of the medium the drug is mixed with. Hence, someone who sells ten grams of pure heroin mixed with eighty-nine grams of sugar is not subject to mandatory sentencing (they are below the 100-gram level), but someone selling five grams of pure heroin mixed with ninety-five grams of sugar faces a five-year mandatory sentence. This kind of idiocy penalizes persons at the low end of the distribution networks, who typically deal in more diluted drugs, disproportionately to those at the higher end. This kind of rule also produces sentencing cliffs such that meaningless differences in amounts can produce significant differences among defendants in terms of penalties.

The mandatory sentencing guidelines were formulated to produce equity so that, among other things, defendants—whether rich or poor, black or white—would all be treated the same (that is to say, equally harshly). This does not seem to have occurred. It is another of those unintended consequences of well-meaning laws. Because judges are forced to use specific sentences, prosecutors have more power to manipulate defendants; they can offer them lesser charges for cooperation. But who has something the prosecutor wants? Certainly not the street user. The people at the bottom end of the scale have little to bargain with. The way this works out is that white defendants will plead guilty and receive motions for reductions of sentence for cooperation more frequently than will black defendants (Meierhoefer, 1992, p. 23). This difference was negligible in 1984 when mandatory sentencing was introduced. In other words, instead of producing the effect of equal treatment under the law, blacks (and Hispanics) were treated even more harshly relative to whites than before the guidelines.

Given that black and Hispanic populations are disproportionately affected, there is a cascading unintended consequence of the war on drugs and harsh prison sentences. These people have families, too. They have wives and dependent children. Mumola (2000) reported that in 1999, 63 percent of federal prisoners (and 55 percent of state prisoners) reported having children under the age of eighteen, and that 46 percent were living with them at home at the time of arrest. Hence, 336,300 households with minor children had at least one parent in prison. Assuming the proportion of prisoners with dependent children is equally distributed across crimes (a shaky assumption), then you would have 195,000 households that have a parent who is in federal detention for a drug-related crime. As it happens, black children are nine times as likely to have a parent in prison than are white children (7 percent versus 0.8 percent), so once again the burden falls on a disenfranchised minority. Hispanic children were also three times as likely to have a parent in prison than were whites (2.6 percent).

THE STATES RESPOND: THE EMERGENCE OF DRUG COURTS

According to Dannerbeck, Sundet, and Lloyd (2002), a shift from viewing drug offenders as criminals to viewing them as individuals in need of treatment within a structured environment has taken place. This has led to the creation of so-called "drug courts." This began as an experiment in 1989 in a Dade County, Florida, circuit court and has mushroomed into a nationwide program, with courts in all fifty states as well as U.S. territories. Not only do these provide an alternative to the criminal justice system for addicts, they provide an important relief valve for the overcrowded courts themselves, since they move people through faster than the standard criminal courts system (Hatley and Phillips, 2001). As of September 2004, 1,212 drug courts were operating in the United States, and 476 more were in the planning phases. Currently, fifty states plus the District of Columbia, Puerto Rico, Guam, one federal district, and fifty-two tribal courts have operational drug court programs (http://www.whitehousedrug policy.gov/enforce/drugcourt.html). Because they are designed to handle only the nonviolent drug offender, they cannot replace the standard criminal court system, but it is clear that they are and will be playing a larger role for selected drug offenders.

No actual uniform standard for the drug courts exists. Ideally, a drug court team will be formed. This consists of a team of professionals that includes the judge, attorneys, a probation officer, and a treatment manager who work together to support the offender (Dannerbeck, Sundet, and Lloyd, 2002). This is a "carrot and stick" type of operation; addicts or users who have a drug problem can get a reduction in sentence, or even have the charges dismissed, in return for an agreement to complete a drug treatment program. However, failure to complete the treatment typically results in the person being sent to jail or prison on the original charges. The perception is that this program would not work without that threat (a perception bolstered by Rempel and DeStefano, 2001).

In 1997 the U.S. DOJ Drug Courts Program Office identified these key components for a successful drug court program (adapted from Listwan et al., 2003):

- integration of alcohol and drug treatment sources with justice system case processing;
- a nonadversarial approach emphasizing teamwork;
- eligible participants identified early and promptly placed;
- participants provided with a continuum of treatment and rehabilitation services;
- abstinence monitored by frequent drug testing;
- compliance and noncompliance coordinated with drug court strategy; and
- ongoing judicial interaction (this last point labeled "crucial").

Judge Peggy Hora (2002), labeling the system "therapeutic jurisprudence," added to that list three more components: continued monitoring and evaluation to gauge effectiveness in achieving goals, continuing interdisciplinary education about addiction theory for the police and officers of the court, and forging partnerships between the court and community-based organizations. The system is perceived as a therapeutic vehicle with the judge at the center of everything controlling the treatments (Goldkamp, 2001).

Hatley and Phillips (2001) examined one specific drug court from its inception in 1994 through 1999 to determine what factors had significant predictive values for success. That is, what are the characteristics of the persons who successfully graduate from the drug court treatment program compared to those who fail to complete treatment? Based on previous research, they chose to measure gender, race, marital status, dependent children, age, and educational background. They also considered employment, in terms of whether they were employed at the time of arrest, provided employment during treatment phase, or kept their employment during treatment. Finally, they coded drug usage by type of drug that sent the clients to the program: alcohol, cocaine, crack cocaine, methamphetamine, heroin, and marijuana. Polydrug use was not measured.

Factors significantly related to drug court success in this review were being white, older, having a high school diploma, and all employment measures. Minority members did not graduate at as high a rate. The other negative predictive factor was being referred for cocaine use. A confounding effect of these two factors (race and drug type) and a compounding age factor are both probable. More recently, Rempel and DeStefano (2001) examined the Brooklyn Treatment Court (BTC) results from 1996 through 2000 and found a slightly different mix of factors. They used a multivariate regression analysis to produce several models of factors and how they influenced outcomes.

Negative outcome indicators were being young, female, less educated, and unemployed, and use of highly addictive drugs such as cocaine or heroin. Positive factors were identified as level of legal coercion in terms of length of sentence waiting if they dropped out, having a family court case pending, and having family or other emotional support. Yet another negative factor was how long after appearing before the court they had to wait for placement in treatment. This, in turn, turned into a confounding variable with gender because female defendants had to wait twice as long for placement (due to less available facilities). The authors suggest the controlling factor here was waiting, not gender, and that the noted sex effect was an artifact. Another positive factor was discovered when the BTC program went from a preplea to postplea format. To enter the program, the participants had to first plead guilty and have an actual jail/prison penalty imposed. This might also have affected the exceptionally high retention rates of those who had prior felony convictions, since they would face a significantly longer sentence if they failed the program.

Overall, just how successful are these programs? It is possible to construct samples of people who are apparently good matches in terms of demographic data and drug use type. Yet, in the end, we are going to be comparing a group of people who have voluntarily entered a program versus those who have either actively rejected that program or who did not have the opportunity to enter the program. This is further compounded by the variations that will exist between courts and jurisdictions. Thus, while comparison studies do exist, finding well-controlled studies that comport to a true experimental design is difficult. Instead, we have quasi- and nonexperimental designs and retrospective studies. Listwan et al. (2003) in reviewing previous studies found ten with positive outcomes (that is, lower recidivism rates or other positive measures for those who completed a drug court program), three with no real difference, and two with negative outcomes. The latter two found a slightly higher probation revocation rate in Chester County, Pennsylvania, and a higher recidivism rate in Las Vegas, Nevada. The Nevada study was conducted by Goldkamp (2001), who found that for all arrests, a higher proportion of drug court graduates were rearrested; however, for specifically drug-related arrests, the rearrest rate was lower than that of the comparison group. Furthermore, this effect was only observed during the last two years of the study (1996 and 1997), which indicates that other factors may have been at work. The study of Listwan and colleagues did not find any difference between drug court graduates and a comparison group in terms of rearrest rates.

Goldkamp (2001) argues that merely looking at rearrest rates is too narrow. What matters more is not whether someone is rearrested, but the length of time between the arrests. On average, when people are rearrested, it takes two to three times as long as a comparison group. This indicates a slowing of criminal activity. This effect alone may be enough to justify the system. It is, after all, a bit unrealistic to think criminal addicts would eliminate all criminal activity just because they have had treatment for their addictions. On the other hand, given the lack of true experimental control and the numerous changes that occur outside the system (such as "three strikes and you're out" laws), the apparent positive effects could be spurious. It is also quite possible that other factors, such as typical risk factors just mentioned, are more potent than the drug court effect itself. It would be easy to read too much into the positive outcomes of the drug courts, but that still doesn't detract from their usefulness.

A reasonable conclusion would be that these programs probably do some good and seldom make situations worse. No doubt, they are cheaper than the regular court system. Rempel and DeStefano (2001) did a cost-benefit analysis of the BTC system. For misdemeanor arrestees, the average savings across participants was $1,320; for first-felony participants the state saved $12,365 and for multiple-felony participants it saved $14,256. The former group would typically be facing six months in jail if they were not in the program; the others from one to one-and-a-half years in jail or prison. The real savings came from a predicate-felony group. These people had prior felony convictions and were facing an average of three years or more in prison. These participants generated an average savings of $57,534! These numbers reflect the difference between costs of providing treatment and running the court versus the costs of incarceration and regular court costs. This also means that drug courts would probably benefit from accepting more serious offenders for the program rather than just first offenders, as some systems do. In a similar study analyzing the cost benefit ratio in Washington, the Washington State Institute for Public Policy estimated the state saved $2.46 for every dollar spent on the system and that a break-even point for the system was achieved at the point at which the fall in recidivism was only 6.6 percent (Washington State Institute for Public Policy, 1999: <http://www.wsipp.wa.gov/rptfiles/drug_court.pdf>).

To give credit where credit is due, the federal government is actively supporting the drug court system. That support comes from the Omnibus Crime Control and Safe Streets Act of 1968, as amended by the Twenty-First Century Department of Justice Appropriation Authorization Act (2002). In 2004 the DOJ awarded $18,139,668 million in grants to support this system. Each grant was limited to a maximum of $450,000 if applied over a three-year period ($200,000 for two-year periods) and needed to have a 25 percent match from local funds (DOJ figures, <http://www.ojp.usdoj.gov/BJA/grant/04drugCTAwds.pdf>). However, we still have a long way to go to maximize the benefits. As U.S. District Judge Ralph Erickson noted in a Minot, North Dakota, speech, the present judicial system will someday be labeled "the dark ages" (AP story published November 23, 2003). He went on to state: "We have money for prison cells, but we should put it into treatment. We are making criminals out of some people who just need lessons."

Since the drug courts are so much cheaper for the system than the standard court approach, and since they provide benefits to the system by helping to mitigate the overcrowding in courts and prisons, ample justification to continue or even expand their use exists. It is probable that the same type of program would work equally well in the federal court system. It seems that the only reason to restrict participants to only nonviolent offenders is a desire to see a violent offender punished for his or her actions. Naturally, the public wants someone who commits a violent crime to receive a prison sentence, and in the case of possible future violence, the public deserves to be protected. But if the drugs are what caused the violent crime, would it not be better to address the root problem, which would also address recidivism, than to insist on punishment for the crime? This option should be available for the special case.

Chapter 6

What Works:
Part I—Education

If locking people up for long periods of time is not going to be sufficient to stop illicit drug use, and if we are unable to successfully interdict the flow of drugs to people who want them, then how can we address the problem? This question really has two answers, and implementing them will do more to win the war on drugs than if we redoubled or tripled the efforts at interdiction or incarceration. Even better, it will do so far more cheaply and humanely than the other strategies. This chapter is focused on education; it examines efforts to convince people not to use drugs in the first place and represents the most efficient use of money to fight the war on drugs. However, not all efforts are going to be equally effective.

Logically, education efforts can be divided into two primary categories. One of them is public proclamations such as public service ads in the media. The other is school-based efforts. These should be natural partners but are actually relatively independent. The former can be, and are, aimed at all segments of the population, while the latter are obviously aimed at children and adolescents. No one questions the need to have such programs; adolescent drug use in the United States is the highest in the industrialized world (Macaulay, Griffin, and Botvina, 2002). The challenge has always been coming up with effective programs. Since they are largely independent of each other, we will begin with the school-based programs.

EARLY EFFORTS

According to Beck (1998), U.S. schools have a long history of drug education in the schools, dating back to the Women's Christian

Temperance Union. Beginning in Vermont in 1882, with support from the National Education Association (NEA), the idea of having a curriculum that included information warning against alcohol, tobacco, and other intoxicating "narcotics" became so popular that within four years it had spread to every state but ten and was mandated at all nationally owned schools and the military academies. This was called "scientific temperance instruction." It was aimed first at alcohol, then at tobacco, and last at other drugs, notably narcotics. The general theme was to describe the evil effects of the drugs and scare people into not using them. No doubt the proponents of this saw the passage of the Eighteenth Amendment as vindication for their efforts.

With the repeal of prohibition, education appeared to enter a new phase. Instead of the trumpeting of the evils of drugs the strategy seemed to be one of silence. Drug education as part of the curriculum seemed to fade away. The next changes occurred in concert with the changes in the political climate as first John Kennedy and then Richard Nixon were elected to office.

In 1963 the President's Advisory Commission on Narcotic and Drug Abuse declared:

> There is a vigorous school of thought which opposes educating teenagers on the dangers of drug abuse. The argument runs that education on the dangers of drug abuse will only lead teenagers to experimentation and ultimately to addiction. The Commission rejects this view. . . . The teenager should be made conscious of the full range of harmful effects, physical and psychological, that narcotics and dangerous drugs can produce. He should be made aware that, although the use of a drug may be a temporary means of escape from the world about him, in the long run these drugs will destroy him and all he aspires to. (pp. 17-18)

This signaled a change away from a "say-nothing" posture. Most of the Commission report dealt with other things, though, and the result was that no coherent program was proposed to produce a curriculum for use in the schools.

Blum (1969) was particularly critical of the education efforts in place through the 1960s. He noted that most school-based education programs were oriented toward scare tactics reminiscent of those used to condemn marijuana in previous decades. That is, the information being presented to students was more propaganda than a factual look at the drugs. Most students of high school and college age, of course, will be resistant to that kind of approach, especially when common sense tells them the reality is not as horrible as what is being presented. They knew of a number of people who used alcohol without becoming alcoholic; they typically knew or knew of other students who used marijuana who were not destroyed by the drug. The typical end result in this situation is that they begin to distrust all information given them about drugs, which hampers their ability to deal with real problems. So here is yet another example of unintended consequences, although this one comes from poorly designed education curricula rather than ill-considered legislation.

Then Richard Nixon won office and proclaimed the now infamous "War on Drugs." One result for education from this was the availability of federal funds to support efforts in the schools. Giving credit where credit is due, finally providing funds for school-based education programs on drugs was a positive step. The initial problem was that the programs were neither well coordinated nor well conceived (Beck, 1998). They were also still based on fear tactics, similar to those used previously in Congressional hearings or public information ads, focusing on the harm that illicit drugs could do. No evidence that they were effective exists. However, another shift of focus that developed in the latter part of the 1970s had some promise.

Swisher (1979) suggested that a series of assumptions concerning drug education existed and that they were becoming increasingly widespread. One was that a reasonable goal for drug-abuse prevention should be to educate people to make responsible decisions regarding the use of all drugs, licit and illicit alike, for all ages. This was a shift away from the goal of scare tactics attempting to prevent all drug use. The second assumption was that responsible decisions would result in fewer negative consequences for the user. The third assumption was that the most effective approach to achieve the goal of reduced drug use would be a program that increases self-esteem, interpersonal skills, and participation in alternatives. This last assumption bears an obvious similarity to the Drug Abuse Resistance Education (DARE) program developed only a few years later.

The Drug Abuse Prevention, Treatment, and Rehabilitation Act of 1979 required that no less than 7 percent of NIDA's Community

Programs budget in fiscal year 1980 and 10 percent in fiscal year 1981 be spent on prevention efforts. The government was finally starting to allocate some money for programs. Much of this was eventually funneled into the DARE program.

THE DARE PROGRAM

The Drug Abuse Resistance Education (also known as Drug and Alcohol Resistance Education) program was invented by a cooperative effort of the Los Angeles Police Department and the Los Angeles Unified School District in 1983. It focused on fifth- and sixth-grade children, attempting to give them the motivational and emotional tools necessary to resist peer pressure to try drugs. The program called for one session per week for seventeen weeks with sessions lasting a maximum of sixty minutes. These sessions were taught as part of the school-day curriculum by police in uniform. The police educators teaching the classes first had to complete an eighty-hour structured training course. The students received a maximum total of seventeen hours (typically less) of instruction per year. The stated end goal was to eliminate drugs by stopping demand.

In 1986 the National Institute of Justice reported some successes of the program. This coincided with First Lady Nancy Reagan's "Just Say No" concept and, with Congress appropriating money for a drug prevention program that earmarked 10 percent to go to programs using police in uniform to teach classes, DARE was launched nationwide (Jodi Upton, *The Detroit News,* February 27, 2000). By 1998 the program was in place in 80 percent of the school districts in the United States (Kalb, 2001). The cost of the program, given its widespread use, was considerable. Shepard (2001) reported that DARE cost between $175 and $270 per student per year. Factoring in training for the educators (police officers), the total national cost was estimated to be between $1.04 billion and $1.399 billion per year. Most of the initial moneys were paid specifically to the program by NIDA grants, but currently the mandated monies are no longer given to DARE.

Few would argue that the program didn't seem like a good idea. It had obvious face validity and it seemed to address what was perceived as a real problem in a practical way. Unfortunately, those early promising results failed to materialize. A number of studies questioned the efficacy of the program. Lynam et al. (1999) did an extensive comparison between pre- and post-DARE attitudes and the effects on behavior. They began with a sample of 1,429 fifth-grade students from a metropolitan area in Tennessee. The students were 75 percent white, evenly divided male and female, and mostly urban. Few were impoverished, although all strata were represented. They were followed at five- and ten-year intervals. The final ten-year sample had 1,002 students, 43 percent male and 57 percent female. Measurements included both prevalence of heavy drug use and frequency of drug use in addition to the attitudes and expectations they had about drugs. They looked at four drugs or drug groups: Alcohol, tobacco, marijuana, and other illicit drugs combined. What they found was discouraging.

Pre- and post-DARE expectations of positive and negative effects of all four sets of drugs were strongly correlated at the ten-year follow-up. That is to say, the program did not do much to alter opinions about the drugs and nothing changed with that across ten years. In terms of actual drug-use behavior, DARE had no measurable effect. Completing a DARE course had no predictive value for later drug use. Two of the goals of DARE were to teach students how to resist peer pressure and to increase self-esteem. The assumption is that these are skills that would allow them to stay away from drugs. This study found no lasting effect in ability to deal with peer pressure and, surprisingly, actually found a negative relationship with self-esteem, although the authors suggest this was an anomaly they don't expect to be replicated. The final conclusion was that DARE had no reliable short-term, long-term, early adolescent, or young adulthood positive outcomes.

This is not an isolated study; many have failed to find evidence that DARE works and virtually nothing indicates it does work. Yet this program still continues around the country. Considering the financial cost, why is it continued? Multiple factors may be at work here, but possibly the main one is that parents *think* it works. They observe that most children who go through DARE do not develop problem drug-use behaviors (even if some experiment with them). What they fail to realize is that most children who *don't* go through the program also fail to develop problematic drug-use behaviors. Due to media attention to the situation, parents believe that drug abuse is much more widespread than it really is. Thus, compared with that perceived norm, DARE seems as if it works. This overestimation of the likelihood of an event because the event receives widespread press is known as the availability heuristic. In addition, it's a kind of "feelgood" activity; who wants to be in the position of telling a school not to use what is a standard nationwide program designed to keep kids away from drugs?

A second reason why DARE continues is that most of the cost of the program is not borne by the school. For the school, it only costs about $30* per student, which is much less than competing programs. A third factor is that, in response to the negative outcome studies, DARE programs are being modified in an attempt to fix the problem. Studies—especially longitudinal studies—take time to complete, so the negative studies are inevitably associated with older versions of the program. Thus, proponents would argue that it works now even if it didn't in the past and that we must give it more time. At some point, however, you have to give up on a program that just can't generate positive outcome data. Luckily, alternatives exist.

The real question that needs to be addressed here is, *why* doesn't it work? Skager (2001) suggests it is because the whole program relies on three false assumptions. These are that kids try drugs because they are naive, that they use drugs to ease negative feelings about themselves, and that they use them because peers pressure them into trying them. The first assumption is patently false. In this day and age, it is hard to believe that ten- to twelve-year-old children don't already know about many of the problem drugs, and it is hard to imagine that they will ignore other, competing material on drugs when they are older. Clearly, we have room for education here but it is not as if we are going to be writing on a blank tablet.

Do children actually get involved because of low self-esteem? Recall that this was an idea that grew in the 1960s. If this were true then one would expect a distribution of drug use different from what it actcually is. Drug use cuts across all social groupings in schools; its not just the shy, unpopular "wallflowers" that use drugs. Indeed, it may even be more common among the popular, successful students. In addition, if drugs weren't distributed among the popular kids, where would the "peer pressure" to use them come from? Certainly

---

*This number and other program costs noted later come from the Drug Strategies publication. (See Lawton [1996] next section.)

the unpopular, out-of-favor groupings of kids are not going to have any social influence on the popular kids.

The concept of peer pressure driving experimentation with drugs is probably the most widespread belief of all. This belief probably results from a confusion between social pressure and simple modeling. People whom we admire have what is called "referent power." We want to be like them and we naturally gravitate to imitating their behavior. Likewise, if we perceive a behavior is common or normal among a social group to which we would like to belong, we will modify our behavior to "fit in" with that group. Even rebels have role models they emulate. Trying to fit in and be part of the crowd, yet be independent and separate from adults and parents, drives the formation of cliques; if prominent members of those cliques use drugs, the other members feel social pressure to do likewise.

Finally, a last component to why DARE doesn't work may be its reliance on police officers to present the program. Some officer-presenters are very effective, and they are trained at considerable cost before they actually present the program. However, who better to teach a child about drugs than the professional teacher who already knows them? Many people feel having uniformed police in the schools is a positive experience in terms of developing a comfort level for the students for interacting with the police, but that does not necessarily translate to effective teaching. It may even prove detrimental in some regards. Rosenbaum and Hanson (1998) found that every additional thirty-six hours of cumulative drug education produced significantly more negative attitudes toward police.

OTHER SCHOOL INITIATIVES

DARE, luckily, isn't the only available program. At least forty-seven other school-based antidrug programs are national in scope, and a number of homegrown methods are used in various localities. One of the problems encountered by local school districts is replicating science-based prevention programs, which sometimes results in local programs that have only marginal effects (Macaulay, Griffin, and Botvin, 2002). Lawton (1996) reported on a review of ten such programs conducted by Drug Strategies, a Washington, DC, non-profit organization. Out of the forty-seven total programs, only six earned a report of A for overall program quality. DARE, which received an in-depth review, was not one of them. The top six, in no particular order, were

1. Michigan Model for grades Kindergarten through eight;
2. Alcohol Misuse Prevention Program for grades six through eight (focused only on alcohol);
3. Life Skills Training for grades six through eight or seven through nine;
4. Project ALERT, a two-year program for grades six and seven or seven and eight;
5. Project Northland for grades six through eight (also focused only on alcohol); and
6. Students Taught Awareness and Resistance (STAR), a two-year program for grades five through eight.

This study was updated and expanded in 1999 and included fifty-two programs. They divided the programs into Comprehensive Health, K-12 Drug Prevention, Elementary/Middle School Drug Prevention, and Middle/High School Drug Prevention.

In the Comprehensive set, the Michigan Model was the clear standout with the top ratings in every category. No other comprehensive program came close. No program received top marks in the K-12 group, and that includes DARE (which did not make the grade). Likewise, no program received with high marks in the Elementary/Middle School set. However, eight programs got an overall evaluation of A in the Middle/High School set. These are the same ones just listed plus Project TNT and Reconnecting Youth. However, the only programs that earned top ratings across all categories covered (matching the Michigan Model) were Project Northland and STAR.

What are the characteristics of a successful program? Nation et al. (2003) did a metareview article drawing from thirty-five published articles, which were reviews that specifically addressed characteristics of effective programs. Their analysis yielded nine principles identified as important to include for program effectiveness. These are further divided into three primary areas. In the following list, the numbers refer to the percent of articles that endorsed the particular principle as important or necessary to include.

Area	Percent Endorsing
Program Characteristic	
Comprehensiveness	83
Uses various teaching methods	83
Theory driven	58
Provides sufficient "dosage"	42
Provides opportunities for positive relationships	33
Matching Programs to Target Audience	
Appropriately timed	67
Socioculturally relevant	67
Program Implementation/Evaluation	
Uses outcome evaluations	42
Has well-trained staff	33

It is interesting to note that of the most important characteristics of effective programs, a well-trained staff had the lowest proportion. This would seem to suggest it is more critical, perhaps, to have an appropriately timed, relevant, and broad program than to have an exceptional staff. The Drug Strategies group that rated the fifty-two school-based programs also specifically listed strategies that were known to be ineffective. These were scare tactics and moralistic appeals, curricula that relied solely on drug information, curricula that worked only on self-esteem but did not provide resistance skills training, and single-shot presentations such as assemblies or testimonials that are not part of a continuing lesson plan.

One of the widely cited positive programs that meets these criteria is the Life Skills Training (LST) program developed in the late 1970s by Dr. Gilbert Botvin. LST received an overall score of A in the Drug Strategies breakdown but the review was not quite as positive as those of the three other highlighted programs. In some conceptual ways, LST is quite similar to DARE. Both fall into the category of "no-use" social skills programs (as do Midwestern Prevention Project, Project ALERT, and Normative Education [Brown, 2001]). LST actually predates DARE, but it never received as much widespread use and only recently began receiving much national attention. The reasons for this are most likely financial; with DARE schools typically pay nothing, but with LST teachers must be trained to present the program.

LST has versions of the program for both elementary and middle school and is designed to span three years, although within each year it can be done intensively or at a slower pace. The elementary program consists of twenty-four thirty- to forty-five-minute class sessions, eight sessions per year. The first year covers all skill areas and the next two years provide booster sessions. The middle school program consists of fifteen forty-five-minute class periods. A booster intervention has been developed that is taught over ten class periods in the second year and five in the third year. This means the initial program should be implemented with sixth- or seventh-grade students, followed by booster sessions during the next two years. The main focus of the program is to teach skills in the areas of drug refusal and personal self-management as well as general social skills. The rationale for this is that poorly competent youths may use drugs to achieve developmental goals they believe cannot be achieved by more conventional means (Botvin and Griffin, 2002). They may also feel overwhelmed when faced with important decisions, such as whether to use tobacco, alcohol, or other drugs.

Macaulay, Griffin, and Botvin (2002) noted that the LST program has consistently produced significant reductions in tobacco, alcohol, and marijuana use. SAMHSA reports these figures from its Model Programs Web site (http://modelprograms.samhsa.gov/template_cf.cfm?page=model&pkProgramID=9):

- reduced initiation of cigarette smoking by 75 percent, and three months after program completion, by 67 percent;
- reduced alcohol use by 54 percent, heavy drinking by 73 percent, and drinking to intoxication one or more times per week by 79 percent;
- reduced marijuana use by 71 percent, and weekly or more frequent use by 83 percent;
- reduced multiple drug use by 66 percent;
- reduced both long-term and short-term substance abuse;
- reduced pack-a-day smoking by 25 percent; and
- decreased use of inhalants, narcotics, and hallucinogens by up to 50 percent.

Botvin and Griffin (2002) also report on a longitudinal evaluation of the program using 6,000 students from fifty-six junior high schools in New York State. The subjects in this study were not very ethnically diverse (91 percent white). More recent studies (but looking only at one year follow-up data) have used urban, ethnically diverse samples. For example, one study measured the program effects for 3,261 students who were 61 percent African American and 22 percent Hispanic (Botvin et al., 2001).

LST, like DARE, is a "one size fits all" type of program. All students in the school receive the same program. It is possible that those who most need such a program will not benefit as much as those who are less likely to use a substance without exposure. Griffin and colleagues (2003) addressed this issue with a study done in New York. They identified teenagers who were "high risk" for developing tobacco use and who received the program ($n = 426$) and compared them against a similar control group who did not receive the program ($n = 332$). High-risk designation was based on level of exposure to substance-using peers and poor academic performance. The results were encouraging. A one-year follow-up showed significantly less alcohol, tobacco, inhalant, or polydrug use among those who had the program, and a nonstatistically significant reduction in marijuana use as well. The cost of the program is around $275 per student.

To date, all studies show the same basic benefits—decreased drug use across the spectrum from tobacco and alcohol to marijuana and polydrug use compared to control groups. In contrast to DARE, substantial published evidence suggests LST has a positive impact. On the other hand, LST is not without its critics. Brown (2001) suggested the evaluation of LST had serious methodological problems, which included questionable methods of combining samples across schools or studies, arbitrary cutoff points for excluding subjects from the final data pool, and failure to report negative results that actually occurred. He went on to note that the actual curriculum of LST was very similar to other "no-use" drug education programs that had been proven ineffective in the past. The report does not suggest that LST is ineffective but does raise concerns that praise for it may be premature.

Another problem with LST assessment studies is that the founders of the program, notably Dr. Botvin, have been involved in almost all the research done to evaluate the program. Again, this in no way suggests the research was flawed or that improper conclusions were reached, but the relative lack of completely independent evaluations is troubling.

The Michigan Model that began in 1984 is a program used at 90 percent of the public schools in Michigan and is more comprehensive than DARE or LST. Drug education begins in grade seven and continues into high school. It is combined with several other health issues, including diet, violence, exercise, and sexually transmitted diseases. Some components of the program, such as sex education, have faced opposition from parents who feel it is too explicit. However, the program is continuing.

Shope, Copeland, and Marcoux (1996), reviewed the effects of the drug curriculum on students who participated in the program for two years. Students received seven lessons on alcohol in grade six and another eight lessons on alcohol and other drugs in grade seven. The researchers found that the rate of substance use (alcohol, cigarettes, marijuana, and cocaine) increased significantly less than it did for the control group. As with LST, the Michigan Model program is taught by regular teachers. Concerning the close similarity among DARE, LST, and the Michigan Model and the inability of DARE to produce such positive results, this may be a crucial factor in a program such as this. The basic cost of the program is $240 per student, which is also generally less than the other recommended programs.

Project Northland and STAR also deserve some attention. Their basic problem is cost. Project Northland costs $549 per student and focuses strictly on alcohol. STAR tops the list at $610 per student. For most school districts with a viable alternative, this cost is going to price them out of the market.

The point of all this is not that some programs have more research to support them than do others, or even that some programs appear to be more effective than others. The crucial point to be made is that research shows that education in the school system can be effective in reducing the level of drug use in teens. Unfortunately, as we will see with treatment, while the system works, it doesn't work as well as we would like it to. Providing antidrug training to teenagers or preteens in the schools will not be sufficient to solve the problems.

PUBLIC EDUCATION

The other branch of education is the effort to inform the general public. Public education consists of public service announcements, which includes public service ads in print media, billboards, and broadcast media, and information offered to the public through various channels such as Web sites. Ads, when used properly, have proven to have great value in curbing alcohol and tobacco use. The value of the latter is as yet unclear. One caveat must be offered here: Public education that offers propaganda rather than real facts, or presents only one side of controversial issues, is not likely to have any long-term positive benefits and may even prove counterproductive.

It is critical that when the government sends a message to the public about illicit drugs only the truth be presented. Otherwise, we run a great risk of those who do know the facts about some particular drug rejecting all messages about all drugs as lies and propaganda. Sadly, this is the position the government is still in with regards to marijuana. As late as March 2003, on the an NIDA Web site (http://www.nida.nih.gov/MarijBroch/Marijteenstxt.html#3), the federal government was telling people that marijuana is addictive and can damage the fetus of pregnant women, suggesting it is a gateway drug for harder substances, and relying on old research to support the idea that it causes long-term memory and thinking impairments. All of this was part of a much larger body of data, which was informative and accurate. At the very least, these "facts" about marijuana are controversial, but presenting only that point of view cannot help but weaken the credibility of the government on other matters.

This problem is highlighted when you visit the Web site maintained by the ONDCP at <http://www.mediacampaign.org/mg/television.html> that focuses on media campaigns. It lists a variety of links to media presentations on drugs and allows us to view newer television ad spots. Twenty-three television ads were available for viewing (in English) on the site in March 2004. Four of them were generic and did not focus on any one drug, two focused on Ecstasy, and the remaining eighteen concerned marijuana. If nothing else, this shows the fixation the government has with marijuana. With all of the other drugs available to teens, some of them extremely dangerous and/or harmful (such as crystal meth), virtually all you get from the ONDCP media campaign is antimarijuana spots. To make matters worse, at least some of these ad spots are obviously inaccurate and attempt to portray the dangers of marijuana as being worse than they really are. This will serve to reinforce the perceptions of people who are unlikely to use marijuana anyway, but the real target audience—young people who are just starting to use the drug or think about it—is unlikely to be persuaded. As soon as teens discern that they are being fed propaganda rather than good, factual information, they are likely to reject the entirety of the ad. An even greater risk is that they will be suspicious about the factual information we are trying to give them about other drugs. It is possible to argue that the libertine attitudes toward LSD and other psychedelics of the 1960s was the natural outgrowth of just such a reaction to the silly propaganda of the 1930s and 1940s concerning marijuana (such as in the movie *Reefer Madness*).

One of the most significant developments in this arena comes from turning the control over the media to the teenagers themselves. Typically, teens will present a harder-edged message to their peers than will adults, and these ads are apparently very effective. In 1998 in Florida, funded by the tobacco settlement money, a campaign was launched under the title "The Truth." The main theme was: "You are being manipulated by the tobacco industry." One of the television ads, featured in a 2004 ABC News documentary titled *From the Tobacco File*, portrays two executives visiting a man in the hospital. They thank the man, who is coughing and struggling for breath, for being such a loyal customer and tell him, "We don't know how we'll replace you." They then walk out into the hall and eye a teenager walking by. The teen looks up at their glare and asks, "What?"

Within just two years smoking among middle school students was reduced by 54 percent, and a 24 percent decline in smoking among high school students occurred (Kilgore, 2000). The project is ongoing and includes a very clever Web site (http://www.thetruth.com/index.cfm?connect=truth). However, it, as with the initiatives of many other states, is under financial pressure. Massachusetts, for instance, went from a robust $50.5 million antismoking budget in 2001 to a paltry $2.5 million for fiscal year 2003-2004 (*Boston Globe*, March 16, 2004). The result was a sharp rise in illegal tobacco sales to teenagers. This might reflect increased demand as well as decreased policing of vendors.

The Massachusetts program had been hailed by many as a model program. Siegel and Biener (2000) published a four-year longitudinal study of the effects of the campaign. They found no effect on youths who were already smokers, and no effects from radio ads or outdoor billboards. However, youths age twelve to thirteen at the study outset who were exposed to the TV ads were significantly less likely to begin smoking than were cohorts who were not so exposed. The results would seem to indicate that these programs should focus on electronic media and be aimed at the early teenager.

Azar (1999) writing as a staff reporter for the *APA Monitor* (a publication of the American Psychological Association), reported on a study that tested 196 antismoking ads on teenagers. These ads were divided into seven categories, but only three categories had any impact. Surprisingly, perhaps, the ads that depicted the dangers of smoking or other health-related issues were among those that didn't work. Those that did were ads that featured peer models choosing not to smoke and who think smokers are misguided, and ads that featured effects of secondhand smoke on the family.

Another state with a positive reputation for its antitobacco and antidrug stance is California. In 1988, the state approved Proposition 99, which raised the tax on cigarettes an additional twenty-five cents per pack. Part of this tax money was used to produce ads designed to reduce smoking. This went further in 1998 with Proposition 10, which increased sales tax on tobacco by fifty cents per pack and earmarked the money for public health issues, including antismoking ads. The media campaigns produced were successful if one can judge by the number of tobacco deaths in California. Already 9 percent under the national rate in 1988, the lung cancer rate in California fell to 19 percent below the national average by 1997, and death from chronic pulmonary disorders went from 1 percent above the national average to 15 percent below in the same time period. It would be impossible to prove that these changes came from public service ads, but it would be naive to conclude that they had no effect. Still, death rates may not be the best measure because death from tobacco use typically takes some years to document.

A better measure is use rates. Goldman and Glantz (1998) present a compelling case for the effectiveness of the media campaigns in California. Prior to the passage of Proposition 99, total cigarette consumption was already falling by 45.9 million packs per year; after passage (and the airing of the antitobacco ads) that rate of decline tripled to 164.3 million packs per year. Even more interesting was what happened when the money for these ads was temporarily cut off. In 1992, claiming the ads were ineffective, Governor Pete Wilson suspended them. Tobacco decline slowed to 19 million packs per year. Wilson was sued, the money was restored, and decline in smoking

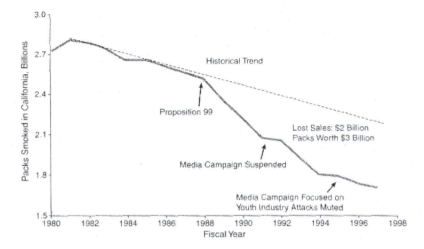

FIGURE 6.1. Relationship Between Antitobacco Media Campaign and Smoking Frequency in California. (*Source: American Journal of Public Health,* 1997, 87(5), 871. Reproduced with permission from the American Public Health Association.)

accelerated again, although it was flat from 1995 to 1997 when no new ads were aired. Verbal description, though, does not do this justice. Figure 6.1 is from the Goldman and Glantz article. Note that before Proposition 99, nothing separated California from the rest of the country. The dramatic change in smoking prevalence in California compared with the national average occurred immediately after the ad campaign began. Looking at a graph such as this, it is difficult to deny the effects of public service advertising on smoking. Because nicotine is among the most addictive of substances (see Chapter 8), we have no reason to doubt that well-produced media campaigns concerning other drugs would be effective.

DRUG-USE TRENDS

Whatever we are doing, we are doing something right. Overall trends in tobacco, alcohol, and illicit drugs are promising, although they are not uniform and some drugs *do* have troubling trends. The Monitoring the Future (MTF) Survey, conducted by the government to monitor drug use in eighth-, tenth-, and twelfth-grade teenagers nationwide, is one of three Health and Human Services–sponsored surveys. The other two are the National Survey on Drug Use and Health, which monitors use of all drugs in the population age twelve and over, and the Youth Risk Behavior Survey for students in grades nine through twelve, which collects a broader range of data than does the MTF survey. The latest published MTF survey, completed in 2003, collected data from 48,467 students from 392 public and private schools. It found significant reductions in lifetime use patterns of any illicit drug—from 41 percent in 2001 to 37.4 percent in 2003. Likewise, past-year use dropped from 31.8 percent to 28.3 percent and past-month use from 19.4 percent to 17.3 percent for the same time period. The best part of this news is the broadness of the reduction in hitting almost every drug measured. This indicates that users are not just substituting another drug for what they are giving up.

Chapter 7

What Works:
Part II—Drug Treatment

Drug education will probably never be completely successful. The very nature of the drugs we are trying to stop is that they are seductive, and some people will never respond to education about them. Hence, addiction and addicts, even if greatly reduced, will remain a problem for a long time to come. What do we do with these victims? Do we just lock them up and forget about them, or is there a better way of dealing with the problem?

The most important fact that needs to be brought out is that *drug treatment programs really do work;* they just don't work as well as we would like them to. The idea that treatment is largely ineffective is a myth. This myth is partially a result of a history of limited success, a reliance in the past on medical models of treatment (which are largely doomed to failure if not combined with some other form of therapy), and the difficulty in treating drug addiction. It may also be an effect of treating drug addiction as an acute medical disorder—one with a sudden onset and rapid recovery when successful—when in fact it is more like a chronic illness such as diabetes that demands long-term care and is characterized by relapse. However, even if not permanently curative, treatment does produce a higher level of benefits than incarceration. McClellan and colleagues (2000) reviewed more than 100 controlled trials of addiction treatments and concluded that most showed significant reductions in drug use, improved personal health, and reduced social pathology. Unfortunately, they reported few or no cures. But if the goals are the more modest ones of lower recidivism rates and cost savings compared to incarceration, numerous studies over the past fifteen years have shown that treatment works. Only when we look back to the 1980s and the years before do the benefits of treatment become questionable.

THE FEDERAL NARCOTICS FARMS EXPERIENCE

Very early on, Congress recognized the need for some form of treatment for drug-addict prisoners. In 1929 Congress passed Public Law 672, which established two "narcotic farms" for confinement and treatment of persons "addicted to the use of habit-forming narcotic drugs" who had been convicted of some crime. This is sometimes referred to as the Porter Bill. One was established in Lexington, Kentucky, and the other in Fort Worth, Texas. These were, in fact, federal prisons, but they were specifically reserved for an addict population and the stated purpose was to cure the prisoner of his addiction.

The Lexington farm opened on May 29, 1935. In 1942, they began accepting neuropsychiatric patients in addition to just addicts. The facility eventually closed in 1974 and the physical facilities were transferred to the Federal Bureau of Prisons (BOP). Fort Worth had an almost identical history, except that it was shorter in duration. It opened on October 28, 1938 and also began accepting psychiatric patients in 1942. It closed in 1971, transferring facilities to the BOP. While in operation, the staff focused on detoxification. The actual treatment protocols employed beyond this were somewhat limited. As a result, they probably did little to lower recidivism rates. This no doubt fed into the myth that treatment is ineffective.

The problem with using detoxification as a treatment protocol and not addressing other problems the addict has is that it equates addiction with physical dependence. The primary motivation for people to use recreational drugs is not to stave off withdrawal symptoms; it is to satisfy a craving for the drug experience. In other words, psychological addiction is a more powerful motivator than physical addiction. Any program that focuses exclusively on physical addiction is therefore doomed to failure. By extension, any program that focuses primarily on detoxification and fails to add some other effective treatment is unlikely to have many positive results.

DRUG-SUBSTITUTION MODELS

These models attempt to replace a damaging substance with one that avoids the problems of the original drug. The program in question here, of course, is methadone maintenance. Methadone maintenance was developed by Dole and Nyswander in 1964. Many would argue that this isn't a treatment at all since methadone is also an addictive narcotic. However, it has properties that make it attractive as a substitute for heroin. Other substitutes for heroin have been used this way, but methadone is far more widely in use than they are, and it has a better overall history of results. It is important to bear in mind that as with detoxification programs it does not really get at the root of the problems for the addict, but unlike detox, it does deal with the critical issue for the addict—the craving.

Methadone is a synthetic narcotic that has a stronger binding to blood plasma than does heroin or morphine. It was developed by Germany in World War II to make up for loss of morphine supplies. A single oral dose can be effective for twenty-four hours. If the dose is adequate it will also block any high the addict would get from a heroin dose yet allow the addict able to function normally (Kleber, 2003). Since dosage is controlled by the clinic, overdoses are rare. However, an overdose is still possible if the client uses something in addition to the methadone in an attempt to get high. The risk of an accidental overdose in new clients also exists, since they may not grasp how long the drug remains active in their system. For this reason, some clinics, such as the state-supported Paseo Clinic in Kansas City, Missouri (one of five methadone clinics in the greater Kansas City area) will not accept new clients just before holidays when the clinic is going to be closed since that would require them to give the client methadone to take at home.

Is the program working? It certainly is widespread. Approximately 170,000 addicts are maintained on methadone. This number is fairly steady across years but with individuals, on average, staying on the drug for only a few years. Some people who go off the program are in long-term remission and may never return to opiate use, while others revert to their habit. A number of addicts need to stay on the program indefinitely (Kleber, 2003). Barnett and Hui (2000) suggest that expanded access to the program produces a cost-effectiveness ratio of less than $11,000 per quality-adjusted life year (QALY). This is more cost-effective than many widely used medical therapies. QALY looks at a combination of cost of treatment and outcome. The lower the number, the more preferred that form of treatment is. U.S. health care systems tend to adopt treatment protocols that produce QALY ratio

costs of $50,000 or less. At a ratio of $11,000, methadone maintenance is a very attractive program.

In Canada, the cost of methadone maintenance in Toronto in 2000
was $6,000 per year, but the estimated cost of an untreated heroin ad-
dict was $44,600 per year (from Health Canada Web page: <http://
www.hc-sc.gc.ca/ahc-asc/alt_formats/hecs-sesc/pdf/pubs/drugs-drogues/
methadone-treatment-traitment_e.pdf>). NIDA recently noted that it
costs about $3,400 per year to maintain an addict on methadone com-
pared to $3,000 for outpatient counseling or $18,000 for inpatient
treatment. All of these options are distinctly cheaper than prison. In
other words, whether looking at quality-of-life improvement measures or just bottom-line dollar costs, methadone maintenance is a
cost-effective way to spend our money.

The metropolitan Kansas City area has five methadone clinics, each
with around 200 clients (Rose Jett, personal communication, 2004). The
typical client is a polydrug abuser and, in Kansas City, they are all self-
referred rather than referred by drug courts. Regular testing is done, and
during treatment clients tests about 80 percent clean from other drug use.
This suggests that the program will reduce the level of abuse of other
drugs in addition to opiates. Surprisingly, only about 60 percent are heroin users. The others use a variety of pharmaceutical opiates including
Oxycontin, fentanyls, and morphine. Similar to most other clinics, they
encourage clients to attempt gradual withdrawal, but if the client feels
they need it, they can stay on the program indefinitely.

Is methadone maintenance a cure? No. After all, the client is still
using an addictive drug. Is it an effective treatment? As long as we do
not demand "drug free" to be part of our definition of "effective," and
as long as we are willing to supply adequate doses to the clients, it is
among the most effective ways of treating narcotic addiction. Furthermore, we can (and should) combine methadone maintenance
with some form of therapeutic intervention. The poorest results are
found in programs that supply minimal doses and no therapy and the
best results are found in programs that add psychotherapy to an
adequate dose of the drug (Carroll, 1998).

MEDICAL TREATMENT MODELS

These are models of treatment that tend to focus on detoxification
with or without an additional drug. As previously noted, they are

largely doomed to failure because they do not take into adequate account how drug addiction differs from a disease. Drug-taking behavior in addicts is driven by cravings, not by the unpleasantness of withdrawal. If the desire is to prevent future drug use, something must be done to address the precipitating factors behind these cravings.

National Public Radio in February 2004 broadcast a series of five programs focused on heroin in the Boston metropolitan area. The treatment program they featured was one based on buprenorphine. This is a synthetic narcotic that can be used for pain relief. It is a partial agonist for morphine (that is, it has some of morphine's narcotic properties but not all of them) and apparently has a stronger affinity for the mu receptor site in the brain that is activated by morphine and heroin than they do. The patient is first switched to this drug to eliminate withdrawal symptoms, then weaned off buprenorphine over a couple of weeks. Following this, the patient is maintained on naltrexone, a pure narcotic antagonist, for six months to two years. Naltrexone is a pure narcotic antagonist and will prevent the patient from getting high even if they choose to take heroin again.

In many ways this treatment protocol is similar to the nicotine patch for smokers. We substitute a different form of drug for the damaging habit and slowly reduce our dependence on this new form. Clearly this will work for some motivated people but, just as clearly, it is not a panacea, and many people are not successful in stopping tobacco use even by using a nicotine patch. Still others revert to smoking at a later point in time. If all we do is provide a way for patients to eliminate narcotics from their systems we have addressed only one of the issues involved in their being an addict in the first place. Despite some early success stories (see Kosten, 2003, for a review) this is not likely to be a viable solution for a majority of users. For instance, a recent Australian study of fifty-one patients who were switched from methadone maintenance to buprenorphine found that 69 percent had gone back to either heroin or methadone within one month of withdrawal from buprenorphine (Breen et al., 2003).

McClellan et al. (2000) argue that the dilemma is that we are treating a chronic problem more like we treat a short-term disease problem. They make an interesting analogy using treatment for hypertension. Note first that both drug addiction and susceptibility to hypertension have genetic components, that voluntary behaviors play a significant role in the onset of the disorder, and that neither is curable by current medical practices. However, each is susceptible to treatment. Imagine if we treated hypertension the same way we treat drug addiction.

> Hypertensive patients would be admitted to a 28-day hyperten-
> sion rehabilitation program, where they would receive group
> and individual counseling regarding behavioral control of diet,
> exercise, and lifestyle. Very few would be prescribed medica-
> tions, since the prevailing insurance restrictions would discour-
> age maintenance medications. Patients completing the program
> would be discharged to community resources, typically without
> continued medical monitoring. An evaluation of these patients
> 6 to 12 months following discharge would count as successes
> only those who had remained continuously normotensive for
> the entire postdischarge period. (p. 1694)

No one would expect this to work for hypertension, yet we expect it to work for drug dependence. Relapse following treatment for hyper-tension is typically considered evidence of the effectiveness of treat-ment, yet relapse following treatment for addiction is considered evidence for the lack of treatment effectiveness.

THE RESIDENTIAL TREATMENT PROGRAM IN FEDERAL PRISONS

In the early 1990s, treatment began receiving serious attention in the federal prison system after languishing in the 1970s and 1980s. The BOP mandated dedicating positions solely to drug treatment at all facilities, identifying all inmates with treatment needs, and devel-oping a delivery strategy that would include education, nonresiden-tial treatment, residential treatment, and transitional care programs. The result of this was the intensive residential treatment program. Participation was voluntary, but addict prisoners were strongly en-couraged to participate, with the result that in 2001 more than 15,000 inmates completed this program. This number has continued to climb, with 16,243 inmates participating in 2002 and 17,578 in 2003 (Ina Winn, BOP, personal communication, April 15, 2004).

The residential treatment program is based on a biopsychosocial model and treatment is cognitively based (Vanyur and Strada, 2002).

It clearly has probative value as a program. Based on 1998 data, inmates who completed the residential drug abuse treatment program were 73 percent less likely to be rearrested and 44 percent less likely to use drugs, compared with similar offenders who did not participate in residential treatment (Vanyur and Strada, 2002). Prisoners in the program, and prisoners who had completed the program but who were not immediately released, also had a 74 percent reduction in misconduct incidents compared to a matched sample not in the program (http://www.bop.gov). The total spent for all forms of treatment for federal prisoners in 2003 was $43,485,000—a veritable drop in the bucket compared to the cost of prison in general. Consider the return on the money spent! To the government's credit, this program is theoretically available to every prisoner in the system who has been a drug abuser. However, treatment in prison is effective only if it is followed with aftercare (Kleber, 2003). Without a halfway house or outpatient program following prison, the positive effects of treatment decay markedly.

OTHER GENERAL TREATMENT
CONSIDERATIONS AND THERAPIES

Drug addiction (whether of alcohol or illicit drugs) cuts across all strata of society and groupings of people. No one treatment approach will ever be universally applicable to such a diverse group, nor will any given treatment approach adequately address the range of addictive substances. What works for one person, drug, or combination of factors will not work for all. For example, when evaluating alcohol-dependent people to formulate a therapy plan, an important consideration is how they personally view the concept of a "higher power." Those who are largely agnostic or atheistic do not respond nearly as well to twelve-step programs such as those used by Alcoholics Anonymous (AA) as do those who profess a strong religious belief (Dennis Elsenrath, personal communication, 2004). The sad truth is that although a number of treatment approaches exist and have been studied, the most widely used programs are not those with the highest levels of empirical support (Carroll, 1998).

Another consideration involves gender. The majority of drug addicts are male and most programs seem to be geared to serve that group. However, demographic differences between male and female addicts other than gender would suggest we need to take different approaches with them. For instance, compared to males, females tend to begin drug abuse at a later age and are more likely to use illicit drugs or alcohol to cope with traumatic life events or to maintain a relationship with an addict. They are also more likely to have already had some psychological counseling and to have experienced sexual and physical abuse (Dannerbeck, Sundet, and Lloyd, 2002). Not only are women more likely than men to have dependent children, but they are more likely to be the sole caretaker for those children. Hence, lack of child care may prove a significant barrier for those who want treatment.

Another factor that may affect the therapy employed is availability. Even in larger metropolitan areas, programs may be full, or the client may be placed on a waiting list for treatment, court mandated or not. Given that any therapy is probably of more value than none, placing the client in a program merely because a space is open can still be beneficial. However, such blanket placements are not likely to produce optimal results.

Miller and colleagues (1998) reviewed forty-one different methodologies with three or more treatment outcome trials and an additional twenty-six methodologies with one or two outcome studies for the treatment of alcoholism. In all they researched 302 outcome studies that treated 59,833 clients. They then calculated a treatment efficacy score for these methods. The more positive the value, the greater the evidence for the treatment being beneficial; the lower the value, the less evidence. Even a negative score does not indicate the treatment is without benefit, but low negative scores do call into question whether that treatment modality should be widely employed. The range was from a high score of +221 for "brief intervention" to –364 for "educational lectures/films." Other very high scores were +145 for motivational enhancement, +120 for social skills training, and +80 for community reinforcement. Mandated Alcoholics Anonymous programs scored a dismal sixtieth out of 67 with a score of –90. Voluntary AA was not included since they do not release their figures. What can we conclude from this? A number of treatments with proven track records of effectiveness are available for treating alcoholism. If one form does not work well with any given client, a host of other methods can still be tried. Again: We have many effective treatments for alcoholism.

Interestingly enough, the twelve-step approach that came from the original AA model has dominated the field of treatment for alcohol for probably half a century and for other drugs of abuse for the past two decades. It is based on a series of steps developed nearly eighty years ago by a recovering alcoholic in Akron, Ohio. It is probably the most familiar of the treatment approaches to the general public. Without question, it has value as a treatment modality, and many people have benefited from having used it. It provides a strong social support network, a drug-free environment, and is affordable. But despite its benefits, does it deserve the place of prominence it holds? It may never be possible to actually answer this question because the anonymous nature of AA precludes the kind of research necessary to properly evaluate it. It is quite possible that other approaches work as well or better than twelve-step programs. Two different types of therapies that could be used in addition to or instead of a twelve-step approach include cognitive-behavior therapies (CBT) and motivational enhancement therapies.

CBT is typically a collaborative approach in which a patient and a therapist agree on goals of treatment and methods of achieving those goals. CBT is based on social learning theory and is used in many forms in the field of psychology. It is by no means limited to treating drug addiction. For the addict, it attempts to integrate assessment with skills training using modeling, operant and classical conditioning, and role-playing to break the cycle of craving and use. An advantage of CBT from the point of view of the agency administering it is that it is a relatively short-term treatment program and, therefore, within the budgets of most facilities. A good general overview of this being applied to cocaine addiction can be found at the NIDA Web site (http://www.drugabuse.gov/TXManuals/CBT/CBT1.html).

Another category of therapies are the motivational enhancement therapies. Miller and Rollnick (1991) have pioneered an approach called "motivational interviewing." In this approach, the client is gently guided through questioning by the therapist to produce an assessment of his or her addiction problem. This approach has been used with some success with both alcohol and heroin addicts. Sanders, Wilkinson, and Allsop (1991) detail how they use the approach to deal with addicts attending a methadone maintenance program. They begin by getting clients to talk about the good side of heroin then gradually lead them into making a personal costs- benefits comparison. The core concept of this approach is to assist clients in producing motivation to change. This by itself will not solve any problems, but it will make it possible to effectively deal with the addiction.

THE VALUE OF TREATMENT

Without trying to specify exactly which treatment protocol is in use, it is still possible to examine the benefits of treatment in a global perspective. Dr. Alan Leshner, Director of NIDA, in testimony before a congressional hearing (U.S. Senate, 2001) first noted that any successful treatment program administered in prison must include aftercare. The effects of in-prison treatment are dramatically reduced without aftercare treatment. When we compare nontreated addicted prisoners with those who have received treatment and aftercare, we see a huge savings. Fully 80 percent of untreated addicts return to their addiction within a year of release, and 70 percent will be rearrested within that year. By contrast, the treated addict's rearrest rate is only 30 percent. Even if these differences disappeared after that year, we would still have a dramatic savings in cost, treating addicts and keeping half of them out of prison for a year or more is better than just recycling them through the system. This brings to light another aspect: a widespread myth that treatment programs must be voluntary to be successful. Mandated or coerced treatment program outcomes are just as positive as voluntary programs (Rempel and Destefano, 2001).

Costs and savings calculations will vary too much from location to location to provide an exact analysis of the value of treatment, but a few specific examples should be enough to illustrate the general principle. One such comparison was provided by the United Nations (2000) when they compared the costs to society for treated versus untreated cocaine addicts. Based on extensive interviews, they calculated that average crime costs per addict in treatment facilities were $20,700 per year. Due to a reduction of drug-abuse-related crime, following treatment a 67 percent drop in cocaine use occurred. In addition, the crime cost per addict had dropped 78 percent to $4,600 per year. Based on treatment costs of $72 per day (which is about the same as simple prison costs), they calculated a cost-benefit ratio of 1.94. This yields a net profit of ninety-four cents per day per addict following treatment, and does not count savings costs of not having the addict in prison.

A second example is provided by Kings County, New York, District Attorney Charles Hynes in testimony before a House of Representatives hearing on July 13, 1999. In 1990, the Drug Treatment Alternative-to-Prison (DTAP) program was begun. This program has a one-year retention rate of 66 percent. Three years after treatment, the recidivism rate for arrests was 23 percent, compared with 48 percent who spent a comparable amount of time in prison on drug-related charges. Of those who managed to find jobs after release, the rearrest rate was only 13 percent. Of 398 graduates of the DTAP program, the costs for treatment were $22.3 million, but the costs for incarcerating the same number in prison would have been $36.6 million, a net savings of $14.3 million. This is just the cost comparison of treatment to prison. If we now add in two other factors, the savings are even greater. We have a 25 percent savings in number of people rearrested. When we rearrest them we have to pay to keep them in prison. Assuming only a one-year prison term, for 100 prisoners that's another $2,648,000 to add to the $14.3 million. Now add in the taxes paid by those with jobs (average $2,000 per year), subtract the police department and court man-hours for those not rearrested, subtract the crime costs associated with someone who would still be using, and the savings obviously continue to mount. Even if treatment is not fully effective, because the treatment costs less than incarceration and because at least some people will respond by staying off the drugs, very significant cost savings can be found here. In addition, inherent savings in helping people overcome disorders rather than punishing them exist.

Chapter 8

The Legalization Debate

It is not difficult at all to make rational arguments for legalizing at least some of the currently illicit recreational drugs. Some people carry the debate even further, arguing for the legalization of all such drugs. Before going on to recommendations we must examine these arguments. To do this, we must have a better understanding of the nature of the drugs we are discussing. You cannot consider legalizing a drug until and unless you understand the dangers that drug poses. Even then you must make value judgments that compare the damage a drug could or likely would inflict on the user or society with the damage done to people or society by keeping it illegal.

DRUG-DAMAGE CHARACTERISTICS

The first step in deciding whether some substance should be legalized is to understand the actual effects of that substance. It is not going to be enough to understand how a given drug alters our mental state; we must also assess damage, both potential and actual, to the individual user and to the social structure. When looking at the user, we also have to remember that damage does not have to be restricted to physical damage—psychological, emotional, and even spiritual damage needs to be considered as well. Likewise, damage to society can cover a lot of ground, such as the impact of drugged drivers, disruption of the family, lost work days, health care costs, crime, etc. This is obviously a challenging task and typically commands a number of pages or chapters in textbooks. Since this isn't the basic focus of this book, what follows is only a cursory overview that should be sufficient for our purposes.

It helps to consider the legal drugs tobacco (i.e., nicotine) and alcohol to gain some perspective. Most people already have a basic understanding of these two drugs in terms of the health risks, although many people do not fully grasp the levels of damage caused by alcohol abuse. To keep things simple I will refer to tobacco as the legal drug, but bear in mind that the actual mind-altering substance that makes tobacco an addictive drug is nicotine.

Tobacco use causes great physical damage at the individual level. Everyone knows of the link to lung cancer. Research shows that tobacco use increases the risk of lung cancer by a factor of about 25:1 and probably causes 95 percent of all lung cancer deaths. It also increases the risk of most other cancers. One estimate is that 47 percent of all cancer deaths of whatever kind are caused by tobacco usage. More important, it is responsible for about half of all cardiovascular disease deaths on an annual basis. When added all up, smoking causes about 20 percent of adult deaths in the United States in addition to numerous nonfatal diseases (Leistikow, 2000). Health care for cancer, and cardiovascular and pulmonary diseases caused by smoking costs tens of billions of dollars per year.

In stark contrast to the personal physical harm that results—other than being addictive—tobacco causes virtually no damage psychologically. The same is true in terms of damage to society; other than the costs of health care paid for by the public or potential cancers or disease from secondhand smoke, it causes virtually no damage because tobacco use does not alter personal behavior. Thus, the major problem with tobacco arises from long-term physical harm to the user. Because of the obvious physical damage it does, sales of tobacco products to minors have been limited. As of yet we have not decided to limit sales to adults on this basis; this is something to keep in mind when considering the arguments used against other drugs. Because secondhand smoke is not only obnoxious to nonsmokers but has the potential to damage others, smoking is progressively being banned as a public activity. With the overall number of tobacco users continuing to decrease, we may someday reach a point at which tobacco will be banned. If that ever happens, it is likely to be in the very distant future, given the powerful tobacco lobby in Congress.

Alcohol, also a legal drug, is quite different in terms of damage. In sharp contrast to tobacco, alcohol damages society as much as it does individuals. It does so by producing dysfunctional family units, violence, accidents of all kinds, lost work days, and crime. Even public health care costs are much higher for alcohol problems. In addition to the great psychological damage produced by alcohol abuse, the physical damage is extensive as well. The diseases of alcoholism, added together, constitute the third leading cause of death in the United States. These include cirrhosis of the liver, gastrointestinal disorders (ranging from ulcers to a malabsorption syndrome that leaves one incapable of absorbing vitamin B from foods), pancreatitis, brain damage, and various cancers. Cirrhosis of the liver constitutes the eighth leading cause of death in the United States and the third leading cause of death in forty- to forty-four-year-old white males. Other sources cause liver disease, but it is likely that 80 percent or more of these deaths are due to excess alcohol consumption. Entire textbooks have been written on the problems of alcoholism and alcohol abuse. Despite all we know about the damages and dangers inherent in excess drinking, it seems very unlikely that we will return to prohibition. One primary reason for this is that the people who make and enforce the laws are just as likely as anyone else in the public to use this drug, and the majority of people not only use it to some degree, but use it safely without damaging themselves or others.

Examined on their merits alone, it becomes obvious that these two drugs (alcohol and tobacco) are legal for *political* reasons, not because they are harmless. To a very real degree, the illicit drugs are illicit for political reasons too, not because they are inherently more harmful than legal ones. In fact, some illicit drugs obviously would be less harmful to the user or society at large even if they were as widely used as alcohol and tobacco. This is a critical point to remember if any positive change is to be made in our policies. The mere fact that we tolerate these two very damaging drugs wreaks havoc with the rationale for banning others. The policies we have that ban many other drugs have their roots in racial/ethnic discrimination. As pointed out in Chapters 1 and 2, the laws against opiates, cocaine, and marijuana were all originally aimed at specific minority groups and not actually based on the drug effects themselves. These policies have been perpetuated over the years for political reasons, not medical ones. This leads to the inevitable conclusion that it will take a political response to get them changed; mere presentation or repetition of facts about the drugs involved will not do the job.

The illicit recreational drugs can be divided into categories by the type of action they produce and can be characterized by the types and levels of damage by category. Within those broad outlines, certain specific drugs may be more or less damaging. The basic categories are stimulants (which would include nicotine), depressants (which would include alcohol), narcotics (opiate type), and hallucinogenics. Some overlap occurs between the hallucinogenic and stimulant categories, but the others are quite independent from one another. Making no attempt to be comprehensive, let's briefly review some of these drugs.

The stimulants are, without question, the most addictive of substances. In mild forms such as caffeine and nicotine they seem harmless, *as typically used,* from a psychological standpoint. However, the strong ones, such as cocaine and the amphetamines, cause disordered thinking and behavior, and the behaviors they produce are damaging to both the individual and society. Addiction to amphetamine or cocaine in any of their forms will ruin a person's life. Surprisingly, in terms of physical damage, they are relatively safe. They rarely cause damage to the body except in the cases of serious overdoses, and even then if one has a healthy cardiovascular system he or she can probably survive it. The exception to this rule is nicotine, which puts strain on the cardiovascular system such that long-term low-level use (what we find with many smokers) leads to premature death. It is also important to note that the other health problems associated with tobacco come not from the nicotine itself but from the way it is used. Tobacco use in any form is seriously damaging, but smoking is notoriously so. Objectively, considered as a class of drugs, stimulants are the ones most deserving of control.

The depressants typically don't cause much physical damage, with alcohol being the exception. Alcohol is a poison to body tissue and if sufficiently abused will cause considerable personal damage. The other drugs in this category, such as barbiturates or the benzodiazepine minor tranquilizers, are addictive and pose significant dangers for an overdose, especially if mixed with another depressant or with opiates. However, they produce little or no physical damage. Any addictive drug will be abused by some people, but abuse of these drugs other than alcohol is not widespread. The major reason for this may be that alcohol is also a depressant drug and it is legal, and its use is widely accepted in the culture. Thus, if one wishes for the recreational effects of a depressant, it's far more likely he or she will turn to alcohol than another variety.

The narcotic opiates, natural or synthetic, are also physically be-nign, causing no damage to the body even when abused for long peri-ods of time. Likewise, they cause no mental damage or psychological deterioration. They do pose some risk to the individual who takes an overdose, but this risk is typically exaggerated in the popular press. If one is addicted to heroin, the most popular opiate class drug for illicit street use, it takes a massive overdose to pose a danger because the tolerance to its depressant effects on respiration builds up so rapidly. In terms of society, if these drugs were legal they would probably pro-duce very little damage. They do not induce behavior changes that can damage others; the worst that can be said of them is that they can produce indolence in certain people, but even that is not a common re-sult. It may well be desirable to control opiates, but if damage control is the object of our endeavors, it is easy to make the case that most of the damage results from the fact that the drug is illegal, not from the actual effects of the drug. Logically, a rational drug policy would place control of narcotics toward the bottom of the list. The one prin-cipal exception are the designer narcotics cooked up in someone's basement laboratory. With no real quality control, and sometimes no real skill, some batches may turn out to be seriously flawed, and the addict that buys the resultant poison will be injecting it directly into their bloodstream. This was the source of the "case of the frozen ad-dicts" in California in the early 1980s (see Hanson and Venturelli, 2001, p. 246). In an attempt to produce a meperidine-like synthetic heroin, too much heat was used. This caused the presence of 1-methyl 4-phenyl 1,2,3,6-tetrahydropyridine (MPTP), which led to severe brain damage when injected.

This leads us to the hallucinogenics. This category contains a real potpourri of substances that range from the relatively benign to seri-ously damaging. These are substances that alter the perceptual pro-cesses of the mind, often producing effects of hallucinations (false perceptions; sensing something that isn't actually there whether it be a sound, such as a voice, visual input, or some other sensory input), delusions (false beliefs), or altered psychological states. Only a few are physically damaging, but it is not possible to categorize this whole class of drugs in terms of whether they are psychologically damaging because some are devastating and others not damaging at all. As a further complication, what constitutes benign and what con-stitutes dangerous is not always entirely clear. Thus, more so than the other three categories, we must examine the individual drugs in this grouping. Other than marijuana, these have remained beyond the scope of this book, but it might be instructive to look at some of them briefly.

Lysergic acid diethylamide (LSD) is the most potent drug we have ever discovered. It causes serious alterations in perception, and people under its influence may partake in strange, sometimes self-damaging activities, such as trying to climb down the side of a building like Spiderman. This is rare, however. Very few people die or even seriously injure themselves because they are acting on a delusion caused by LSD. Despite its potency, no one has ever died of an overdose. It is not addictive either psychologically or physically, and it causes no known physical damage to the user. It's the extreme potency of it along with the serious levels of perceptual alteration that make this a scary drug for many people. Another worrisome aspect is that the drug can produce a "recurrent reaction," known by most people as a flashback. This is an LSD-like experience that happens to about 5 percent of users, during which they "trip out" despite not having taken another dose of the drug. The good part is that use and abuse is largely self-limiting, since when people have a bad experience with it they typically stop using it. Thus, whether this is a dangerous drug that needs to be controlled is somewhat controversial.

Compare that with phencyclidine (PCP), sometimes known as "angel dust." It is typically grouped with hallucinogenics but its actual classification is that of a dissociative anesthetic. If ever a drug deserved the appellation "killer drug," this has to be it. It causes some users to have extremely violent episodes, during which they will feel no pain and after which they will have a retrograde amnesia. As any police officer will tell you, they really don't want to have to arrest someone who is "dusted." PCP may cause permanent brain damage as well. A mini-epidemic occurred in the early to mid-1970s, probably because PCP was fairly novel at that time and was very cheap. This didn't last because word of its damaging effects filtered down through the illicit drug-using community. Still, no matter how dangerous a substance is, some people will always use it, so it still exists on the market.

Now take these two examples and compare them with marijuana. What we quickly discover is that they might as well be from completely separate categories of drugs. However, so much nonsense has been written about marijuana in the popular press—ranging from the newspaper horror stories of the 1930s to the popular magazines of the 1980s and 1990s—that it is no wonder the public is confused. Marijuana is a mild hallucinogen that causes some alteration of sensory functions, but typically not so much as to interfere with normal functioning. The exception to this is in the ability to operate machinery; people are no more competent to drive a car or run other machinery under the influence of marijuana than they are when under the influence of alcohol. In terms of psychological dangers, it seems to be the most benign of all the illicit substances, causing no damaging alteration in personality or behaviors. Realistically, it is not any more psychologically addictive than caffeine and is not at all physically addictive. Perhaps partly because of its apparent mildness and safety combined with its widespread availability, it has become and remains the most widely used and experienced of all the illicit substances, reaching into every strata of society.

With this in mind, one has to wonder why marijuana continues to receive such bad press. The answer to this question is probably dependent on the concept of marijuana as a "gateway drug." One of the most widely cited dangers of marijuana is that it serves as a gateway to more dangerous substances. In other words, the reason why some people travel down the slippery slope of drug addiction with "hard" drugs was that they began experimenting with marijuana. The implication is that had marijuana not been used fewer people would have become users of even worse drugs. That claim, though very widely believed, is false.

First, numerous studies have failed to support that allegation. If marijuana were truly a "gateway" drug, it ought to be simple to demonstrate the effect. Instead, all we have is the statistical relationship that most "hard" drug users tried or used marijuana before graduating to the worse drugs. However, statistics and correlations must be interpreted with caution. Among the most recent studies looking at this connection was one published by Morral, McCaffrey, and Paddock (2002). Using the NHSDA data, they were able to construct a statistical model that accurately predicted levels of hard-drug use where presence or absence of marijuana was not a relevant factor. In other words, marijuana use did not change the risk factors for getting involved in other drugs. The reason why marijuana use *seems* to be associated with hard-drug use is that opportunities to use it consistently precede the opportunities to use other, harder drugs, often by many years. Therefore, if someone has any propensity to use illicit drugs, it is very likely that the first one will be marijuana, as nothing else is as readily available. In fact, a 2002 National Center on Addiction and Substance Abuse survey reported that teenagers found buying marijuana easier than buying tobacco (*Narcotics Enforcement & Prevention Digest*, 2002b).

This bears some emphasis. First, no solid evidence for *any* illicit drug serving as a gateway drug exists. Most specifically, *no sound evidence that marijuana is a gateway drug for any other illicit drug exists.* Any suggestion that marijuana use in some way *causes* increased use of other drugs comes from spurious conclusions based on correlational data. Many people do not really understand that a correlation between two items does not prove that one causes the other. If you correlate age with vocabulary size for fifteen- to thirty-year-old people, you will find a very strong positive result. Does that mean that getting older causes you to learn new words? Not really. If you were on a desert island with no books to read and no one to talk to during that time, your vocabulary would not improve. It is because of your life experiences that your vocabulary grows, not because you get older. If we want to get silly about this, when it comes to drug use, we can do much better than point to a correlation between marijuana use and later use of other drugs. One substance was used compulsively by *every single illicit drug user* well before they used any illicit drugs, typically many years before: milk. What's even worse is that fully *half* of all people who drank milk as an infant now score less than the national average on standard intelligence tests. "But," you may say, "the analogy doesn't work because milk is not a recreational drug." Well, perhaps not. On the other hand, consider that those who were involuntarily deprived of their milk actually cried when it was withdrawn, and the user shows palpable enjoyment during its use. Joking aside, the point should be clear that just because Activity A reliably precedes Activity B does not, and logically cannot, prove that A in some fashion *causes* B or that B would not have occurred had A not taken place.

What seems to make marijuana a gateway drug is that the same social and psychological factors that lead a person to experiment with marijuana will be the culprits behind experimenting with more dangerous drugs. The real truth is that tobacco is far more important as a gateway drug than marijuana; virtually every illicit drug user starts using tobacco before using any of the illicit drugs, including marijuana. If this is what makes a drug a gateway drug, and if we could stop other drug use by closing such a gateway, then logically we could solve the whole panoply of illicit recreational drug use by seriously cracking down on underage tobacco use.

None of this is really new data. One of the most distressing problems in trying to formulate rational policy is the tenacity with which certain false conclusions remain in the minds of lawmakers and the DEA. Administrator Asa Hutchinson of the DEA stated as recently as 2002 that "Marijuana continues to be the most widely abused and readily available illegal drug in the United States and *a 'gateway' to the world of illegal drug abuse*" (*Narcotics Enforcement & Prevention Digest,* 2002a, emphasis added). In truth, the worst that can be said of marijuana is that it probably causes similar physical damage to the user as tobacco does. No credible evidence suggests it is addicting, even for fairly heavy users. Yet, as we learned earlier, for largely political reasons, this remains a Schedule I drug completely banned by the federal government for any use. The only chink in that armor has come from the Ninth Circuit in California, where a federal appeals court has refused to overturn a December 2003 ruling that allows Californians to grow and use marijuana for medicinal purposes. On June 6, 2005, the United States Supreme Court ruled to overturn the Ninth Circuit decision. The effect of this was to free the federal government to continue to prosecute the medical use of marijuana.

The next factor to consider is addiction. Addiction can be of two types: Physical addiction produces a set of physical symptoms when use of a drug is suddenly terminated. This is called withdrawal. The reason withdrawal occurs is that the brain has made internal adjustments to compensate for the effects of drugs on the body and when the drug is no longer present these compensations produce an unbalanced state. Depending on the drug and the depth of addiction, and depending on whether a person eases withdrawal with the use of an alternate drug, full physical withdrawal can last from a few days to several months, and can range from unpleasant to life threatening. Eventually, though, if the process doesn't kill the addict, he or she can get back to his or her original state of functioning. (Note: Alcohol withdrawal can kill; heroin withdrawal cannot.) Physical dependence is not a permanent condition, although it can reassert itself rapidly if the user goes back to the drug that caused it. Examples of physically addictive drugs include depressants such as alcohol and opiates such as heroin.

Psychological addiction results from a craving. This craving also results from a change in the brain, but it is not the same kind of change that produces physical dependence. Ex-smokers, or smokers who have tried to quit, are familiar with drug cravings. Some people can manage to ignore them, and some cannot. In any case, it is these cravings, not the physical withdrawal, that really drive drug-dependent behavior. Hanson and Venturelli (2001) produced a chart of how addictive various drugs are in terms of ease of becoming hooked and difficulty of giving them up. A score of 100 indicated maximum addiction potential; lower numbers are relative values to that nominal score of 100. If you have never seen something like this, it might surprise you:

Nicotine	100
Smoked methamphetamines (such as "ice")	98
Crack cocaine	96
Crystal methamphetamine (injected)	90
Valium	85
Alcohol	82
Heroin	80
Cocaine	75
PCP (phencyclidine)	60
Marijuana, Ecstasy, mescaline (peyote), psilocybin ("magic mushrooms"), or LSD	<20

Notice that the top three scores belong to inhaled stimulants. Also, note that marijuana and the other hallucinogens are not very addictive if, in fact, they are addictive at all. Cocaine HCl (75) is probably much more addictive than alcohol (82) initially, but it is easier to give up; hence, it has a final score very close to that of alcohol. These kinds of numbers are available from many sources, which makes the government's incessant focus on the addictive nature of marijuana use even more difficult to understand.

With this in mind, I propose that the most commonly abused illicit substances (currently legal drugs are not considered here) be rank ordered this way, the most dangerous or damaging drugs listed first and grouped:

> *Group I: Seriously dangerous*
> Methamphetamine—inhaled forms such as "ice"
> Crack
> Phencyclidine (PCP)
> Cocaine other than crack
> Amphetamines other than those that are inhaled, including crystal meth

> *Group II: Moderately dangerous*
> Methaqualone (quaaludes)
> Barbiturates, such as Seconal
> MDMA (Ecstasy)
> Opiates, including heroin

> *Group III: Not very dangerous at all*
> LSD
> Marijuana

This is based on combining addiction potential with damage to the individual (both physical and psychological) and damage to society, and then making some judgments on the type of damage induced. In other words, this listing is my own personal opinion about how dangerous various drugs are; other well-informed people may have a different opinion. It is also not a complete listing of illicit recreational drugs and ignores both alcohol and tobacco, both of which would go near the top of this list if included (although for different reasons). Notice that the most dangerous drugs are dominated by stimulants because of the changes in behavior they induce, but that stimulants are not very physically damaging as a rule and are not physically addictive. If we restricted ourselves to medical use only, heroin would drop down even further in the list.

In a rational world, we would attach penalties and enforcement efforts to a list such as this by spending the most on the worst drugs and the least on the safest. This seems unlikely to happen, but it still might be possible to construct a compromise position that takes into consideration some of these damage factors. The real problem in constructing a position is deciding what kind of damage gets what kind of weight. That is, what is more important: a shortened life span from physical damage caused by the drug, or changes in personality or behavior that threatens the well-being of the user and others around him? In concrete terms, both alcohol and tobacco cause physical damage, but alcohol also causes behavior changes that make some people more aggressive and more willing to act out on aggressive impulses.

Another problem we must address is whether the damage is primary (caused specifically by the drug itself, such as cirrhosis of the liver caused by alcohol abuse) or secondary (caused by the response of society to the drug). Heroin, for instance, will not damage your body (other than an overdose or an overdose caused by mixing drugs). However, since heroin must be bought from illicit sources, users do not receive a pure drug and are unlikely to take it under sterile conditions or in a controlled manner. Therefore, the argument is that the physical damage to users results primarily from the legal response to heroin rather than any action of the drug itself. Making it legally available (perhaps through physicians or clinics) might result in less total damage even if it also resulted in more use and more accidental overdoses. These are all issues for which you will find reasonable people on both sides.

Numerous opinions on the subject of legalization have been published. Perhaps the strongest advocate for changing things is Ethan Nadelmann, director of the Lindesmith Center, a drug policy research center. Goldberg's (2002) book presents essays pro and con on a number of drug-related issues. Legalization is the very first issue covered. Nadelmann is pitted against Eric Voth, chairman of the International Drug Strategy Institute. However, Nadelmann is hardly a lone voice; the book includes a number of other well-recognized advocates for change, including the conservative writer William F. Buckley Jr., former mayor of Baltimore Kurt Schmoke, noted (some would say notorious) psychiatrist Dr. Thomas Szasz, and Yale Law School Professor Steven Duke. Balancing out these opinions are the general weight of public opinion and the official position of the various drug control agencies. Specific issues within this debate interact and overlap with one another, but we will attempt to focus on a few directly.

HEALTH ISSUES

One of the principal benefits touted by the pro-legalization group is that a net gain in health would result. Users must buy their product from unregulated sources. They never know what they are getting, nor can they be sure of strength. A heroin addict you expect to get a packet that is 20 percent pure and receive one that is half that or double that. Dose calculation for optimal effect becomes problematic. Even worse, when users buy heroin it is almost a certainty that it has been "stepped on" by adding adulterants, some of which could be very harmful. Finally, users may not have access to a clean needle for injection. Result: Serious health risks are associated with this habit, all of which are caused not by heroin but by the fact that it is an illegal drug. If it were legal to use this, users would be able to get the product from a reputable pharmaceutical company, would know precisely what they were taking, and would no doubt have access to sterile modes of delivery.

Heroin offers the most dramatic example because it is most commonly used by intravenous (IV) injection and is never found pure on the street. Any other drug taken by injection that did not start out as a legal drug will produce many of the same kinds of health consequences. Perhaps the only exception to this rule are "Mexican reds," which are secobarbital capsules legally manufactured in the United States, legally shipped to Mexico where they enter the black market, and then smuggled back to the United States for sale. At least with these users user knows exactly what they are getting. Another health risk associated with illicit drugs—violence—might not seem to be a health problem on first glance. This is really a double-edged sword since some drugs, such as stimulants, can induce users to behave violently. Still, the main source of violence associated with the illicit drugs comes from the drug traffickers who are at war with one another and the authorities. As Schmoke (1988) suggests, decriminalization would remove most of the profit from dealing in illicit drugs and greatly reduce the violence we currently associate with drugs. Consider alcohol prohibition and the violence associated with bootlegging, a specific kind of violence that quickly dissipated with repeal of the Volstead Act.

THE "LEVELS OF USE" ARGUMENT

One of the classic arguments against legalization is that if a drug were legal, then more and more people would use it. It is very difficult to refute this argument when we consider the widespread use of alcohol and tobacco. However, when we look deeper into that criticism, what seems to worry people most is that youths, or teenagers, will be using dangerous drugs at higher and higher rates, creating a nation of addicts. A partial answer to that particular argument is found in a survey done by the University of Maryland (reported in Gray, 1998, p. 291). High school students reported the most difficult drug to obtain was not marijuana but alcohol (not that alcohol is all that difficult to obtain). Why would marijuana be easier to get than a drug that virtually permeates our society? The answer is obvious: alcohol distribution is controlled through government-regulated businesses, but those who control the distribution of marijuana are not so constrained. Furthermore, even when we take into account taxes (which can represent more than half of the retail cost of the final product), alcohol is still so cheap that a black-market product will have a difficult time competing.

A much more compelling argument against legalization comes from the drug-court experience (see Chapter 5). As noted by Rempel and DeStefano (2001), the level of legal coercion strongly correlates with treatment success. Any rational drug policy *must* focus first and primarily on harm reduction. Keeping addictive and damaging drugs illegal therefore serves the purpose of assisting addicts to complete court-mandated treatment programs. Is that a sufficient justification? It is at least a rational reason. However, the argument only works when applied to harmful substances that are addictive and damage the user or society. It seems unconscionable to lump relatively harmless substances in with truly dangerous ones and treat them all the same.

Another factor must be considered: America may be socioculturally different from the rest of the world in terms of recreational drugs. One of the reasons for the passage of the Harrison Act was worry over the rapid growth of opium use in the United States. If we examine drug use today we discover that America has a great deal more drug use than other places. Is there something special about the American culture that leads young people into experimenting with and using dangerous drugs? It is this kind of factor that makes comparisons with other countries somewhat suspect. Nevertheless, in terms of the argument about levels of use, if a drug were legal (or easy to obtain), it may be quite instructive to look at the Netherlands and Europe.

The policy in the Netherlands allows for purchase of cannabis products openly in "coffee shops." Despite this, their rate of marijuana use—either in terms of lifetime use or past-month use—is about one half that of the United States. (For information on this with references, see <http://www.drugwarfacts.org/thenethe.htm>.) When the Netherlands first instituted the policy of allowing coffee-shop sales of marijuana, an influx of foreign visitors occurred, but the local population showed very little change in terms of use. Hence, a form of legalization of marijuana in Europe did not cause a huge increase in use in that population. This may not hold true for America, but it does question the assumption that use would rise dramatically. The Netherlands also allows for a clean-needle-exchange program and, probably as a consequence of that, has a much lower incidence of AIDS victims than the rest of Europe, although the proportion of people using intravenous drugs is about the same as the rest of Europe.

MYTH AND COUNTERMYTH:
THREE BOGUS ARGUMENTS

In testimony before a House Congressional hearing ("Pros and Cons of Drug Legalization, Decriminalization and Harm Reduction," June 16, 1999), a document written by Robert Maginnis was read into the record. This listed eight "myths" supposedly perpetuated by the pro-legalization crowd. A myth is a belief system based on false, incomplete, or nonexistent data. An example of a myth would be what are called urban legends (UL), such as the one that suggests alligators are living in the New York City sewer system. Myths are believed because people want to believe them, either because they fit with their belief and value systems already, or because they seem like an interesting fact. The alligator UL is believable for many people because few actually venture into the sewer system (therefore limiting personal knowledge) and it is easy to believe that people might flush a live baby alligator they obtained while on vacation to Florida down the toilet when they return home. The story gets spread by word of mouth and it grows into a UL. Those who propose myths or ULs often do so with complete sincerity. The same is true of both sides of the drug legalization debate. Much of what both sides present as factual is based on speculation or on bogus research. Without trying to be comprehensive, the following are three of the more commonly cited myths. If you discover that something you thought was true is labeled a "myth," don't feel bad. A common feature of these myths is that the majority of people believe them.

Myth: If you legalize illicit drugs, one result will be a massive increase in usage, because almost everyone who tries them will become addicted. The truth is that the majority of people who experiment with addictive drugs do not become addicted, and that is true of the whole range of drugs, legal and illegal. Most people who take a drink sometime in their lives do not become alcoholics, and most people who have tried smoking at some point in their lives do not become addicted to tobacco, either. This is not to minimize the problem: If 10 percent of drinkers become alcoholic, that produces a massive problem. It doesn't take a huge proportion of people developing problems from a drug to be a major concern if we are dealing with large enough numbers. However, it cannot be denied that many people experiment briefly with illicit drugs and never reach a point of abusing them. The stimulants have the highest addiction potential, but they are not "as high as 75 percent" as reported by the Maginnis testimony before Congress. If it were, since nicotine is acknowledged as the worst offender, then 75 percent or more of all people who have ever smoked a cigarette would become addicted. This is a figure that is obviously false on its surface. Furthermore, in many places in the world drugs are easier to obtain than they are in the United States, yet they don't have the massive addiction problem postulated. Whatever social or other constraints keep people from abusing drugs now will almost certainly continue to operate if the drug were to become legal. So although some increase in use is to be expected, a massive rise in addiction is just speculation.

Countermyth: If we legalize the illicit drugs we won't see much change in levels of use. This, too, is based on pure speculation. No one has really tried this experiment, other than with alcohol prohibition, and even that does not serve as a good model since it took a widely used legal drug, made it illegal, then made it legal again. We could turn to the Netherlands for an example, but that example also is flawed due to cultural differences.

Myth: Legalization would produce an increase in crime. The rationale for this belief is that since a strong correlation exists between illicit drug use and crime, if more people use the drug legally more crime will result. This is specious reasoning. Few drugs alter people in such a way that they become criminals. The closest we could come to supporting this notion would be by using the example of anabolic steroids, which are used to quickly build muscle mass in athletes and can cause them to become more aggressive. It is true that a large proportion of people who commit murder or violent crimes test positive for drugs; but the drug they test positive for is typically alcohol. Indeed, alcohol turns out to be more closely associated with drug-induced crime than anything else. The crimes that are associated with the illicit drugs occur not because the drug alters users' minds to make them into criminals, but because the drugs are illegal to obtain, very expensive because they are illegal, and remain very desirable to have by the users regardless of the sanctions imposed on their use. The users need a great deal of money to support their habits. Unless they have well-paying jobs, and most of them don't, they turn to crime to obtain it. If the drug were legal, and presumably much cheaper, most of the crime associated with drugs would disappear. Hence, it is not the drugs that lead to crime; it is the legal status of the drugs that leads to crime.

HARM REDUCTION

The most rational goal of any approach for dealing with recreational drugs is obviously that of the greatest reduction of harm for the greatest number of people. If all of the damaging recreational drug use stopped, we would achieve this by definition. However, such a goal, however desirable, is not realistic. Recreational drug use is never going to disappear entirely. We have to deal with the reality that harm to individuals and society from drug abuse will continue.

The intrinsic policy problem is that we have no universal consensus on what constitutes harm, let alone which harm is the greater harm. For instance, one form of harm-reduction practice is needle-exchange programs, by which addicts are able to get clean hypodermic needles for personal use. This reduces the risk of HIV or other infectious diseases. Yet, some people have the perception that giving clean needles to addicts only encourages them to use. The reality, of course, is that the addict is going to use the drug anyway, clean needles or not. Therefore, needle-exchange programs are good public policy. Until the public is convinced that they are not increasing the levels of narcotic use, they are not going to be widely implemented.

Methadone maintenance is another way to reduce harm. In this case, the public is generally supportive. These programs allow the addict to control the craving for the drug and to maintain a more productive lifestyle in mainstream society. Since the public sees the benefits of the program, a number of methadone maintenance clinics exist around the country.

When we start to consider legalization issues, the discussion becomes more complex. Consider, for instance, the debate over marijuana. If we assume that marijuana is damaging to the individual, then we will want to limit the use of that drug. To do that, we need to impose controls. At the moment, marijuana is completely banned by federal law. This limits the harm the drug can do to the individual by minimizing the levels of use, and if use by individuals harms society, it limits that harm as well. However, at the same time, harm is done to society due to these limitations; resources must be used to control the drug, and individuals who use anyway and get caught are harmed since they now have a criminal record and are subjected to fines or even prison time. So where is the greater harm? To a large degree, that depends on one's opinion of the dangers of marijuana. Even if we manage to reach a consensus on the level of damage caused by its use, a solution probably still won't be obvious.

This example can be repeated for all of the recreational drugs. Most of them cause harm of some nature, but which harm is the worse harm, and what do we do to try to limit that harm? In other words, how should we allocate our resources to achieve the greatest good? These are murky issues with no simple answers.

CONCLUSIONS

Legalization arguments are easiest to support for nonaddictive substances that do not harm the body or cause the individual to harm others. Even when these substances carry some risk factors, such as potential lung damage from long-term marijuana smoking or the potential of someone on an LSD trip to hurt themselves, the harm inflicted by the law on the fabric of society and on the lives of users should easily outweigh other considerations. Most hallucinogens, but not all, fall into this category. Specifically, marijuana falls into this category. It is not rational to treat marijuana users the same way we treat cocaine users. This is probably the biggest weakness of the current system—the legal response to various users of different substances is substantially the same (notwithstanding differences in sentencing guidelines for dealing in specific amounts of specific drugs) regardless of the true harm or dangers of the drugs involved.

In the final analysis, we are left with a moral question: Just how bad (evil) is drug use? The answer to this question should not get caught up in the false distinction between the currently legal addictive drugs alcohol and tobacco with the currently illicit addictive drugs such as heroin or cocaine, or even the nonaddictive drugs such as LSD or marijuana. In terms of addiction, harm to the user, and/or harm to society, there seems to be no rational reason for the legal dichotomy we currently have. If it is evil to use heroin or allow its use, then it is evil to use tobacco or allow its use. If we are not bothered that people have the right to smoke and drink, then we should not be bothered by giving people the right to snort, toke, or shoot up. Is increased levels of use and addiction (the probable outcome of legalization) combined with a reduction of violence and drug-induced death a worse evil than continuing a system that doesn't work and causes harm of a different kind? These arguments get very tricky at this point because we have no universal agreement on the relative values associated with the various potential harms. The argument seems to be moot anyway, since legalization is very unlikely to occur in the foreseeable future.

On balance, the arguments favoring legalization are stronger than the arguments for maintaining the current system. However, one factor trumps these arguments for dangerous substances: Without the current system that threatens legal penalties for selling or using certain substances, we lose a major source of motivation to get addicts to enter and complete treatment programs. If harm reduction is the goal, then having a system that sends more and more people through treatment, even against their will, is more likely to approach that goal than is a system that does not force treatment compliance. It is for this reason alone that I do not advocate making all, or even most, illicit drugs legal.

This book is restricted to an examination of opiates, cocaine, and marijuana, so it would not be fair to enter a discussion of the entire range of recreational drugs at this point. However, with regard to marijuana, the government would be well served to reverse its course and make it legal for adults, just as cigarettes are. After all, the laws against the drug were based on fallacies, not on factual evidence, and it has not been possible to shake the official government position that continues to support some of those fallacies. Politically, however, this is unlikely to happen. Other ways of making changes exist, and Recommendation 2 in Chapter 9 addresses this point.

Chapter 9

Recommendations

Current U.S. drug policy can best be described as pouring money down a rat hole. We have locked ourselves into a position in which more and more money is spent each year in an attempt to stem the flow of drugs into the country and to prosecute and punish those who break the law. No matter how much we spend or how much effort we put out, it hasn't worked. One droll definition of insanity is to continue to try the same responses to a worsening situation over and over, expecting somehow that outcomes will be different next time. This is as good a definition as any for our national policy on illicit drugs—insane. It brings up a point that needs to be made and repeatedly stressed: By any realistic measure, we are not winning the "War on Drugs." Our current approach has a history of failure and is continuing to fail. Even a cursory examination of the ONDCP 2001 Annual Report on performance measures demonstrates how dismal the record is. Figures B7 through B12 in that report plot the ambitious goals of the government against actual figures and easily demonstrate a complete separation between what is supposed to be happening and reality. Therefore, no matter how attractive it may seem to simply redouble our current efforts, the only sane action is to find a new strategy. It is also necessary to understand that recreational drugs are here to stay. No magic bullet will win a "War on Drugs"; a drug-free America is just not a reasonable goal.

It would be nice to wave a magic wand and revisit the decisions of the past and choose a different path than we are currently on. We might have chosen not to pass the Harrison Narcotics Tax Act and attempted to address the problems caused by opiates differently from the way in which we did; we might have chosen to ignore marijuana, or to treat it in a fashion parallel to alcohol or tobacco products; we might have chosen not to ban heroin for even medical purposes, leaving it a Schedule II drug. I suspect that even with its successes, most people would say we should not have banned alcohol and that the cure turned out to be worse than the problem. However, we can't turn back the clock. We must deal with the current situation. The question is, what shall we do about it?

In one sense, it is likely that nothing drastic will happen in the foreseeable future. As Erich Goode (1999) points out, the current laws stake out an ideological point of view. For many people, they reflect moral and ethical values and these values are not likely to change. The idea is to get people to understand that we *can* do things differently; that we *don't* have to wreak vengeance on every malfeasant to maintain the same moral position. In other words, somehow we must convince people that substituting treatment for punishment is not going "soft" on drugs.

The biggest waste of money would seem to be the resources we spend on benign substances. It was noted at the outset and in Chapter 8 that the purpose of this book was not to present a case for the legalization of any given drug. Nevertheless, no reasonable person can deny that some drugs are far more damaging and harmful than others. A rational policy should seek to limit harm from substances by directing the most efforts and resources at the worst drugs and spend correspondingly less on substances that do less damage. Another way of saying this is that our policies should parallel actual harm related to the drugs instead of supporting the irrational notion that all illicit drugs are equal. That latter position is basically a *moral* judgment that ignores reality. To some small degree, we have managed to make such a distinction in the past by allowing the legal use of alcohol and tobacco (even though the damage done by them should place them at or near the top of the list of drugs that should be controlled). To give credit where credit is due, the government has spent and is continuing to spend significant resources to convince people to either not use alcohol or tobacco, or to use them moderately. These efforts have paid off and continue to pay off. With more resources to use on such efforts, it could be assumed the payoff would be even greater. For our purposes, these efforts also serve as a model for how we might choose to deal with the illicit drugs.

RECOMMENDATION 1:
RESTRUCTURE PRIORITIES

The goal should always be to provide a structure that minimizes damage to both individuals and society from recreational drug use. To that end, the most obvious thing to do, in a perfect world, would be to completely criminalize both alcohol and tobacco. This is not going to happen. However, our response to these two drugs provides us models for how to deal with other drugs (especially the antitobacco campaigns). We have made significant inroads into damaging tobacco use, most notably among adults and less notably among teenagers. We are also starting to see some positive effects on problem drinking. How did we do that, and can we do that with the illicit drugs as well?

The answer for alcohol and tobacco was, and continues to be, education. Education can take many forms, ranging from public service ads in the media to drug education units mandated in school classrooms. If our primary target is teenagers (and it probably should be for education efforts), then another idea is to give teenagers the resources to develop antidrug programs and the creative control over their content. No dollar spent here is completely wasted and the money spent on education has the potential to repay society many times over. Hence, the recommendation is to fully fund these efforts with federal money, whether that be new money or money reallocated from nonworking areas of our war on drugs.

RECOMMENDATION 2:
STOP MIXING APPLES AND ORANGES

We treat the various illicit drugs as if they are from one batch of the same evil. Even if sentencing guidelines recognize the differences between a joint of marijuana and a gram of heroin, our enforcement efforts seem equally aimed at both. Some drugs are worse than others; some drugs cause more harm than others. The logic that it is the harmful drugs that should draw the attention of most of our efforts is inescapable. We should take whatever drugs are deemed illegal and instead of trying to treat them as if they were all equal, concentrate

efforts relative to their dangers. The logical continuation of this principle is addressed in the following paragraphs.

Don't Send the Federal Government
After Marijuana

When the government banned alcohol with the Volstead Act, it
took a Constitutional amendment. That was because it was taking
control over what was otherwise a states'-rights area. When Prohibition was repealed, it took another Constitutional amendment. Contrary to popular belief, the Twenty-First Amendment did not legalize
alcohol; it simply turned the question of legalization back to the individual states. Some states and some counties within states remained
"dry." When the Marihuana Tax Act was passed in 1937, the majority
of states already had laws regulating or banning marijuana. Today,
laws in all fifty states ban marijuana, although some states have decriminalized small amounts of it and some have legalized medical
marijuana.

The current official views of marijuana are still holdovers from
propaganda circulated seventy years ago. Failure to take official note
that the basis for banning marijuana is a moral position and not based
on drug effects perpetuates a form of insanity and is itself morally
reprehensible. If marijuana were actually the "devil weed" it was
originally made out to be, it would make sense for the government to
continue efforts to control it on a national level. If marijuana were actually a gateway drug that induced further illicit drug use, it would
make some sense to focus attention on it. Since it is neither of these
things, why waste money on the problem? In the same way that the
Twenty-First Amendment turned alcohol back to the control of the
states, we should repeal the Marihuana Tax Act and all subsequent
federal marijuana legislation and simply allow individual states to
regulate it. This is not a call for legalization of the drug, since it is not
anticipated that any state will repeal all of its marijuana laws. Since
some states, notably the Western ones, now wish to have marijuana
decriminalized for small amounts and wish it to be legal for medical
use, this would also produce some discrepancy between states in
terms of what is legal or what penalties are imposed. However, this
seems to be a minor problem compared with wasting time and resources by trying to control it on a national level. At the very least,

marijuana should be shifted from a Schedule I drug to a Schedule II drug so that it could be prescribed by a physician, but that change, although logical, would not address the problem as a whole and is not sufficient to have much benefit.

RECOMMENDATION 3:
STOP WASTING MONEY

What is an example of wasting money? Perhaps one is spending large sums of money on attempting to seize drugs as they cross the borders. If we stopped these efforts, it wouldn't change drug availability very much at the street level. By interdicting some smuggled drugs we manage to raise the price of the drugs on the street and we keep some fraction of the drugs from reaching their intended target. However, as has been addressed earlier, we are intercepting only a fraction of the material coming in, which is not enough to keep it out of the hands of even small numbers of users. If that is all we can do—intercept a token percentage of smuggled drugs—perhaps the efforts we are making to interdict them should be token as well. The position being recommended here is not an abandonment of interdiction but a moderation of efforts. We could go back to doing cursory searches, being aware we are not catching much in the way of the traffic, but still forcing those who would break the law to go underground. If someone brings in heroin, cocaine, or some other banned substance on their person or in their baggage and is caught by a cursory search, then we can confiscate the drugs and impose legal sanctions on him or her. However, we would save a lot of money that is being spent for very little positive benefit by reducing our efforts in this regard. The money saved could then be redirected to some other avenue that potentially has a larger impact. That is the point: find the most efficient way to use resources to confront the problems caused by illicit recreational drugs. As noted in Chapter 3, we spend about two-thirds of our money attempting to affect the supply side of the equation, and only one-third on the demand side. Reversing those numbers would be a far more rational way to spend money.

RECOMMENDATION 4:
EXPAND EDUCATION

The most efficient way to handle unwanted behavior is to convince the individual involved not to attempt the behavior in the first place. There may be numerous ways to do this, including having penalties so severe that no one would dare to take the chance, but it seems that some people will always want a thrill. Some people cannot be convinced to not start using various drugs; that is, we will never eliminate our problems with mere threats of penalties. Realistically, the same could be said of education; no matter how much information you give people, some people will not heed your efforts. But people *are* educable. If you provide people of any age group with understandable and accurate information it is likely that the majority, perhaps even the great majority (who would otherwise be attracted to some individual drug experience) will choose not to experiment with that drug. Not only will you be saving that individual from a potentially disastrous personal choice, you will also be saving the nation significant resources it would need to stop that potential drug use. You don't need to stop the traffic in drugs to people who are not going to use the drugs.

The age group that is most likely to begin experimenting with illicit drugs are teenagers and young adults. Peer-group interactions matter a great deal for this demographic. If enough people in the target population reject specific drug usage, this can eventually become a self-sustaining effort. How do you contact these people? Public service ads in the media are good, especially if properly geared toward the audience (such as the "Truth" antitobacco ads in Florida), but the real place to reach them is through the schools. The earlier the effort starts, the better. For this to work we are going to need to provide real education about drugs, not just some simplistic categorization of drugs as evil. As noted in Chapter 6, several proven school-based initiatives exist. These can be improved and strengthened. We should spend money on research to improve these programs and to fund the better ones so that local school districts don't have to foot the bill. We should also drop programs that can't produce measurable results (such as DARE).

One of the biggest problems in mounting a media campaign is keeping politicians away from the money once it is raised. A number of initiatives passed by states to fund antitobacco campaigns have fallen by the wayside when the state "needed" the money for something else. My own state, Wisconsin, basically sold off all of its tobacco settlement money. It was supposed to trickle in over a number of years and, theoretically, was to be used to fund health initiatives to counteract disease expenses caused by tobacco. Instead, the state took it as a much smaller lump-sum payout to balance the state budget for one year. The money was used up on a one-time politically motivated temporary fix of a problem that had nothing to do with why the money was available. This is extremely shortsighted but also a common occurrence. Oregon did something similar in 2003. For education efforts to work, we need a strong commitment that the money designated for education is not going to be redirected into other channels, even when it seems politically attractive to do so.

RECOMMENDATION 5:
FULLY FUND TREATMENT

Treatment *does* work. It can take many forms, and some approaches may work better than others, but it generally is effective. As stated before, it simply doesn't work as quickly, dramatically, and completely as we want it to. One problem in accurately evaluating how effectively we are spending our money on treatment is that we don't give addicted persons a real chance to let it work. We don't tell people that if they have dieted to lose weight in the past and not been successful that they can't try again; we encourage them to try again. We don't tell people who are attempting to stop smoking but who relapsed, "Too bad. You didn't stop forever but went back to smoking, so you can't enter a smoking program again." Neither should we make it a "one shot or too bad for you" situation for illicit drug users. Many, if not most, people who go through drug treatment programs will relapse. We should not discard these people simply because they failed to stay off drugs; we must encourage them to try to quit again.

Congress saw the desirability of providing treatment for heroin users as early as 1929 when it passed legislation creating the "narcotic farms." The first one was established in Lexington, Kentucky, and the second in Fort Worth, Texas. Unfortunately, for the numbers of people involved, these facilities were woefully inadequate, and treatment programs in the middle of the century were not well developed and proofed. Therefore, the results from these treatment programs were discouraging. Therein lies the difficulty; we have shown as a society that we will spend any amount to punish wrongdoers and warehouse them in prison, but rarely spend even inadequate amounts for simple measures, even proven ones, that would make it unlikely they will return to prison. This almost seems to be a characteristic of our society—millions to treat problems, but only pennies to prevent them. We will spend millions to treat the long-term medical consequences of rubella (German measles) for those who develop rheumatic heart disease, but won't fund a federal program that guarantees vaccination for every child. The fact that we are actually headed down the right path—spending larger and larger sums to support education and treatment—is a reassuring sign; we just need to reach the end of that path sooner.

RECOMMENDATION 6:
IMPLEMENT DRUG COURTS
AT THE FEDERAL LEVEL AND ELIMINATE
MANDATORY SENTENCING GUIDELINES

Either aspect of this recommendation could be implemented independent of the other and both aspects should be implemented even if considered separately. They are joined here as one recommendation since they are natural partners of each other. The state-court experience has amply demonstrated the value of putting drug offenders through a drug court as an alternative to a prison term. No reason exists for why this can't be done in the federal system. In fact, the simplest way to implement this would be to use the state facilities already in place for their participants and repay the state for the added costs. One or more sessions of the court could then be designated as drug-court sessions and the same federal judge could handle this as well as regular sessions.

Mandatory sentencing clogs the system and removes discretion from the hands of the judge (and gives it to prosecutors). This does not do much to deter crime; it certainly isn't going to clear up the drug trafficking problem. The reality is that mandatory sentencing is a political stance to slake the public's thirst for vengeance. In the absence of evidence to the contrary, we need to abandon this mode of thinking and focus on what really is effective.

CONCLUSION

Will following these recommendations fix all of our problems, win the "War on Drugs," and turn America into a veritable Garden of Eden? I am not quite that naive. No matter what we do as a society we will still have criminals and crime, drug abusers and addicts, and people who waste their lives on activities that make no sense. Not only can we not legislate morality, we can't even socially engineer positive behavior for everyone. However, we can make things better. We can start to address in a rational fashion problems *created* by our attempts to solve other problems. I firmly believe that if these recommendations were adopted, or if changes that parallel these recommendations were adopted, our society would be better for it and it would not take a microscope to see the difference.

Appendix I

TABLE AI.1. Federal Agencies and Budgets for FY 2002

Department	Amount
Department of Agriculture	29.0
Department of Defense	1,009.0
Department of Education	660.0
Department of Health and Human Services	3,864.0
Department of Interior	39.0
D.C. Court Services	86.0
The Judiciary	820.0
Department of Justice	8,140.0
Department of Labor	79.0
Department of State	833.0
Department of Transportation	591.0
Department of the Treasury	1,547.0
Department of Veterans Affairs	709.0
Corporation for National and Community Service	9.0
Small Business Administration	3.0
Housing and Urban Development	9.0
ONDCP	533.0
Total Federal Drug Budget Enacted	18,960.0

Source: http://www.gpoaccess.gov/usbudget/fy03/pdf/bud32.pdf.

Note: Numbers are in millions of dollars. Compare categories with Table AI.2.

TABLE AI.2. Federal Agencies and Budgets for FY 2003-2005

	FY03	FY04	FY05
Agency	**Budgeted**	**Enacted**	**Requested**
Department of Defense	905.9	908.6	852.7
Department of Education	644.0	624.5	611.0
Health & Human Services	3,315.2	3,479.5	3,656.8
Department of Homeland Security	2,040.0	2,382.9	2,519.4
Department of Justice	2,429.8	2,482.7	2,749.9
ONDCP	520.6	522.2	511.0
Department of State	874.3	914.5	921.6
Department of Veterans Affairs	663.7	765.3	822.8
Other	3.4	2.2	3.5
Total Federal Drug Budget	11,396.9	12,082.4	12,648.7

Source: Executive Office of the President, Office of National Drug Control Policy, National Drug Control Strategy: FY 2005 Budget Summary. Washington, DC; also available at http://www.albany.edu/sourcebook/pdf/t115.pdf.

Note: Numbers are in millions of dollars. Note that the federal budget really didn't reduce the expenditures on the war on drugs by $7 billion between 2002 and 2003; the change was merely one of bookkeeping.

Appendix II

TABLE AII.1. Heroin Addict Numbers and Seizures, 1960-1967

Year	Number heroin addicts	Number new H addicts[a]	Seized heroin (kg)	Estimated illegal imports (kg)[b]	Percent seized
1960	44,906	7,400	183.267	1229.302	0.1491
1961	46,798	7,000	40.259	1281.095	0.0314
1962	47,489	6,400	87.793	1300.011	0.0675
1963	48,535	7,446	83.182	1328.646	0.0626
1964	55,899	10,012	45.110	1530.235	0.0295
1965	57,199	6,012	38.270	1565.823	0.0244
1966	59,720	6,047	31.430	1634.835	0.0192
1967	62,045	6,417	14.656	1698.482	0.0086

Source: "Traffic in Opium and Other Dangerous Drugs." U.S. Treasury Department, Bureau of Narcotics, 1961 through 1968.

[a]Numbers for 1960-1962 are estimates.
[b]Based on 75 mg/day use; does not include "dabblers."

TABLE AII.2. Heroin Addict Numbers and Seizures, 1988-2000

Year	Hard-core addicts	Estimated dabblers	Total heroin seized (kg)	Estimated illegal imports (kg)[a]	Percent seized
1988	923,000	170,000			
1989	886,000	150,000	1,293	24,254.250	0.0533
1990	797,000	140,000	669	21,817.875	0.0307
1991	681,000	395,000	1,432	18,642.375	0.0768
1992	630,000	304,000	1,233	17,246.250	0.0715
1993	694,000	230,000	1,481	18,998.250	0.0780
1994	795,000	281,000	1,268	21,763.125	0.0583

Year	Hard-core addicts	Estimated dabblers	Total heroin seized (kg)	Estimated illegal imports (kg)[a]	Percent seized
1995	855,000	428,000	1,524	23,405.625	0.0651
1996	917,000	455,000	1,343	25,102.875	0.0535
1997	935,000	597,000	1,588	25,595.625	0.0620
1998	980,000	253,000	1,448	26,827.500	0.0540
1999	977,000	484,000	1,137	26,745.375	0.0425
2000	977,000	514,000			

Source: Johnston, P., Rhodes, W., and Carrigan, K. (2000). "Estimation of Heroin Availability 1995-1998." Washington, DC: Office of National Drug Control Policy.

[a]Based on 75 mg/day use; does not include "dabblers."

Appendix III

TABLE AIII.1. Purity and Price: Heroin

City	Purity	Price/mg pure
East		
Atlanta	49	$1.36
Baltimore	27	$0.32
Boston	56	$1.00
Chicago	20	$0.67
Detroit	51	$0.74
Miami	21	$1.10
New Orleans	40	$2.24
New York City	57	$0.98
Newark	68	$0.33
Orlando	50	$0.72
Philadelphia	73	$0.40
San Juan	46	$0.39
Washington, DC	28	$0.66
West		
Dallas	13	$1.39
Denver	18	$1.01
El Paso	42	$0.45
Houston	11	$1.53
Los Angeles	16	$1.00
Phoenix	41	$0.36
San Diego	45	$0.26
San Francisco	10	$1.87
Seattle	8	$1.95
St. Louis	14	$3.52

City	Purity	Price/mg pure
Correlation Eastern cities purity/price		−0.155
Correlation Western cities purity/price		−0.72
Overall correlation purity/price		−0.52

Source: http://www.usdoj.gov/dea/pubs/intel/03023.

Appendix IV

TABLE AIV.1. Purity and Price: Cocaine HCl

City	Price/gm	Purity
Birmingham, AL	$100	NA
Boston, MA	$60	50-60%
Chicago, IL	$125	NA
Columbia, SC	$100	NA
Denver, CO	$100	20-50%
Detroit, MI	$70-$125	60-90%
Honolulu, HI	$100-$120	NA
Los Angeles, CA	$80	80-85%
Memphis, TN	$100	40-50%
Miami, FL	$40-$60	80-90%
New Orleans, LA	$25-$150	NA
New York, NY	$28-$30	75%
Philadelphia, PA	$100-$125	60-80%
Portland, ME	$80-$100	30-70%
Seattle, WA	$80-$100	57-58%
Sioux Falls, SD	$80-$100	NA
Washington, DC	$100	20-60%

Note: NA = data not available.

Source: http://www.whitehousedrugpolicy.gov/publications/drugfact/pulsechk/fall2001/powder.html.

Appendix V

TABLE AV.1. Federal Bureau of Prisons Statistics, 1970-2002

Year	Total sentenced and unsentenced population	Total sentenced population	Total sentenced drug offenders	% of sentenced prisoners who are drug offenders
1970	21,266	20,686	3,384	16.3
1971	20,891	20,529	3,495	17.0
1972	22,090	20,729	3,523	16.9
1973	23,336	22,038	5,652	25.6
1974	23,690	21,769	6,203	28.4
1975	23,566	20,692	5,540	26.7
1976	27,033	24,135	6,425	26.6
1977	29,877	25,673	6,743	26.2
1978	27,674	23,501	5,981	25.4
1979	24,810	21,539	5,468	25.3
1980	24,252	19,023	4,749	24.9
1981	26,195	19,765	5,076	25.6
1982	28,133	20,938	5,518	26.3
1983	30,214	26,027	7,201	27.6
1984	32,317	27,622	8,152	29.5
1985	36,042	27,623	9,491	34.3
1986	37,542	30,104	11,344	37.7
1987	41,609	33,246	13,897	41.8
1988	41,342	33,758	15,087	44.7
1989	47,568	37,758	18,852	49.9
1990	54,613	46,575	24,297	52.2
1991	61,026	52,176	29,667	56.9
1992	67,768	59,516	35,398	59.5

Year	Total sentenced and unsentenced population	Total sentenced population	Total sentenced drug offenders	% of sentenced prisoners who are drug offenders
1993	76,531	68,183	41,393	60.7
1994	82,269	73,958	45,367	61.3
1995	85,865	76,947	46,669	60.7
1996	89,672	80,872	49,096	60.7
1997	95,513	87,294	52,059	59.6
1998	104,507	95,323	55,984	58.7
1999	115,024	104,500	60,399	57.8
2000	123,141	112,329	63,898	56.9
2001	131,419	120,829	67,037	55.5
2002	139,183	128,090	70,009	54.7

Source: Maguire, K., and Pastore, A. (Eds.). (2002). *Bureau of Justice Statistics Sourcebook of Criminal Statistics.* Washington, DC: U.S. Department of Justice.

Notes: Average total sentenced prison population 1973 to 1983 = 22,280; proportion sentenced for drug-related crimes 1973 to 1983 = 26.24%; average total sentenced prison population 1983 to 1993 = 40,235; proportion sentenced for drug-related crimes 1983 to 1993 = 44.98%; average total sentenced prison population 1993 to 2002 = 94,832; proportion sentenced for drug-related crimes 1993 to 2002 = 58.66%.

Bibliography

Anslinger, H.J., and Gregory, J.D. (1964). The Protectors. New York: Farrar, Straus and Company, Inc.

Azar, B. (1999). Antismoking ads that curb teen smoking. *APA Monitor,* 30(1).

Barnett, P., and Hui, S. (2000). The cost effectiveness of methadone maintenance. *Mount Sinai Journal of Medicine,* 67(5-6), 365-374.

Baum, D. (1993). Tunnel vision: The war on drugs, 12 years later. *American Bar Association Journal,* 79, 70-77.

Beck, J. (1998). 100 Years of "Just Say No" versus "Just Say Know": Reevaluating drug education goals for the coming century. *Evaluation Review,* 22(1), 15-45.

Belenko, S. (Ed.) (2000). *Drugs and Drug Policy in America: A Documentary History.* Westport, CT: Greenwood Press.

BLTC Research (2005). The plant of joy. Available online at: http://opioids.com/red.html.

Blum, R., and associates (1969). *Students and Drugs: Drugs II—College and High School Observations.* San Francisco: Jossey-Bass.

Booth, M. (1996). *Opium: A History.* New York: St. Martin's Press.

Botvin, G., and Griffin, K. (2002). Life skills training as a primary prevention approach for adolescent drug abuse and other problem behaviors. *International Journal of Emergency Mental Health,* 4(1), 41-47.

Botvin, G., Griffin, K., Diaz, T., and Ifill-Williams, M. (2001). Drug abuse prevention among minority adolescents: Posttest and one-year follow-up of a school-based preventive intervention. *Prevention Science,* 2(1), 1-13.

Brecher, E. (Ed.) (1972). *Licit and Illicit Drugs.* Boston: Little and Brown, pp. 3-134.

Breen, C., Harris, S., Lintzeris, N., Mattick, R., Hawken, L., Bell, J., Ritter, A., Lenne, M., and Mendoza, E. (2003). Cessation of methadone maintenance treatment using buprenorphine: Transfer from methadone to buprenorphine and subsequent buprenorphine reductions. *Drug and Alcohol Dependence,* 71(1), 49-55.

Brown, J. (2001). Youth, drugs and resilience education. *Journal of Drug Education,* 31(1), 83-122.

Carroll, K. (1998). "Treating drug dependence: Recent advances and old truths." In *Treating Addictive Behaviors,* Second Edition (W. Miller and N. Heather, eds.). New York: Plenum Press.

Choy, Shawn (2002). In the spotlight: Sendero Luminoso. Center for Defense Information Web page: <http://www.cdi.org/terrorism/sendero.cfm>.

Dannerbeck, A., Sundet, P., and Lloyd, K. (2002). Drug courts: Gender differences and their implications for treatment strategies. *Corrections Compendium,* 27(12), 1-8.

Dixon, R. (2003). "Opium production spreading in Afghanistan." *Los Angeles Times,* October 5. Available at <http://www.opioids.com/afghanistan/opium-economy.html>.

Dusek, D. and Girdano, D. (1993). *Drugs: A Factual Account,* Fifth Edition. McGraw-Hill, pp. 215-245.

Falco, M. (1996). "U.S. drug policy: Addicted to failure." *Foreign Policy,* 102. In *Taking Sides,* Fifth Edition (R. Goldberg, ed.), 2002. Guilford, CT: McGraw-Hill, pp. 28-36.

Faupel, C., Horowitz, A., and Weaver, G. (2004). *The Sociology of American Drug Use.* New York: McGraw-Hill.

Federal Drug Control Programs (2002). "The budget for fiscal year 2003." Washington, DC: Executive Office of the President, pp. 379-380.

Galliher, J., Keys, D., and Elsner, M. (1998). *Lindesmith v. Anslinger:* An early government victory in the failed war on drugs. *Criminology,* 88(2), 661-681.

Goldberg, R. (2002). *Taking Sides: Clashing Views on Controversial Issues in Drugs and Society,* Fifth Edition. Guilford, CT: McGraw-Hill/Dushkin.

Goldkamp, J. (2001). Do drug courts work? Getting inside the drug court black box. *Journal of Drug Issues,* 31(1), 27-72.

Goldman, L., and Glantz, S. (1998). Evaluation of antismoking advertising campaigns. *Journal of the American Medical Association,* 279(10), 772-776.

Goldstein, A. (2001). *Addiction: From Biology to Drug Policy,* Second Edition. Oxford U. Press, pp. 235-328.

Goode, E. (1993). *Drugs in American Society,* Fourth Edition. New York: McGraw-Hill, pp. 355-356.

Goode, E. (1997). *Between Politics and Reason: The Drug Legalization Debate.* New York: St. Martin's Press.

Goode, E. (1999). *Drugs in American Society,* Fifth Edition. Boston, MA: McGraw-Hill, pp. 381-418.

Gray, M. (1998). *Drug Crazy.* New York: Random House.

Griffin, K., Botvin, G., Nichols, T., and Doyle, M. (2003). Effectiveness of a universal drug abuse prevention approach for youth at high risk for substance use initiation. *Preventive Medicine,* 36, 1-7.

Hanson, G., and Venturelli, P. (2001). *Drugs and Society,* Sixth Edition. Boston, MA: Jones and Bartlett, pp. 4-27; 60-82; 95.

Hatley, R., and Phillips, R. (2001). Who graduates from drug courts? Correlates of success. *American Journal of Criminal Justice,* 26(1), 107-119.

Herer, J. (2000). *The Emperor Wears No Clothes,* Eleventh Edition. Van Nuys, CA: Ah Ha Publishing.

Hora, P. (2002). A dozen years of drug treatment courts: Uncovering our theoretical foundation and the construction of a mainstream paradigm. *Substance Use and Misuse,* 37(12-13), 1469-1488.

Hynes, C. (1999). *The Decriminalization of Illegal Drugs: Hearing Before the Subcommittee on Criminal Justice, Drug Policy, and Human Resources of the Committee on Government Reform.* 106th Cong., 1st sess., July 13, 1999.

Johnson, B., Golub, A. and Fagan, J. (1995). Careers in crack, drug use, drug distribution, and nondrug criminality. *Crime and Delinquency,* 41(3), 275-295.

Johnston, P., Rhodes, W., and Carrigan, K. (2000). *Estimation of Heroin Availability 1995-1998.* Report prepared for ONDCP by Abt Associates, Inc. Cambridge, MA.

Kalb, C. (2001). DARE checks into rehab. *Newsweek,* 137(9), 56.

Kilgore, C. (2000). Teen antismoking campaign sparks decline in use. *Family Practice News,* May 15. Available at <http://www.efamilypracticenews.com>.

King, R. (1972). *The Drug Hang-Up: America's Fifty-Year Folly.* New York: W. W. Norton.

Kleber, H. (2003). Pharmacologic treatments for heroin and cocaine dependence. *American Journal on Addictions,* 12(suppl2), S5-S18.

Kosten, T. (2003). Buprenorphine for opioid detoxification: A brief review. *Addictive Disorders and Their Treatment,* 2(4), 107-112.

Lawton, M. (1996). New guide gives A's to six of 47 national antidrug programs. *Education Week,* June 12.

Leistikow, B. (2000). The human and financial costs of smoking. *Clinics in Chest Medicine,* 21(1), 189-197.

Liddy, G. (1980). *Will.* New York: St. Martin's Press.

Lindesmith, A. (1965). *The Addict and the Law.* New York: Vintage Books, Random House.

Listwan, S., Sundt, J., Holsinger, A., and Lortessa, E. (2003). The effect of drug court programming on recidivism: The Cincinnati experience. *Crime and Delinquency,* 49(3), 389-411.

Litrell, J. (1995). The beliefs predicting support for heroin legalization. *Journal of Drug Issues,* 25(4), 649-668.

Lynam, D., Milich, R., Zimmerman, R., Novak, S., Logan, T., Martin, C., Leukefeld, C., and Clayton, R. (1999). Project DARE: No effects at 10-year follow-up. *Journal of Counseling and Clinical Psychology,* 67(4), 590-593.

Macaulay, A., Griffin, K., and Botvin, G. (2002). Initial internal reliability and descriptive statistics for a brief assessment tool for the Life Skills Training drug-abuse training program. *Psychological Reports,* 91(2), 459-462.

Maris, C. (1999). The disasters of war: American repression versus Dutch tolerance in drug policy. *Journal of Drug Issues,* 29(3), 493-510.

McClellan, A., Lewis, D., O'Brien, C., and Klebar, H. (2000). Drug dependence, a chronic medical illness: Implications for treatment, insurance, and outcomes evaluation. *Journal of the American Medical Association,* 284(13), 1689-1696.

McWilliams, John (1990). *The Protectors.* Cranbury, NJ: Associated University Presses.

Meierhoefer, B. (1992). *The General Effect of Mandatory Minimum Prison Terms: A Longitudinal Study of Federal Sentences Imposed.* Washington, DC: Federal Judicial Center.

Miller, W., Andrews, N., Wilbourne, P., and Bennett, M. (1998). "A wealth of alternatives: Effective treatments for alcohol problems." In *Treating Addictive Behaviors,* Second Edition (W. Miller and N. Heather, eds.). New York: Plenum Press.

Miller, W. and Rollnick, S. (1991). *Motivational Interviewing: Preparing People to Change Addictive Behavior.* New York: Guilford Press.

Morral, A., McCaffrey, D., and Paddock, S. (2002). Reassessing the marijuana gateway effect. *Addiction,* 97(12), 1493-1504.

Mumola, Christopher (1999). *Substance Abuse and Treatment, State and Federal Prisoners, 1997.* Washington, DC: U.S. Department of Justice, Bureau of Justice Statistics.

Mumola, Christopher (2000). *Incarcerated Parents and Their Children.* Washington, DC: U.S. Department of Justice, Bureau of Justice Statistics.

Musto, D. (1972). The Marihuana Tax Act of 1937. *Archives of General Psychiatry,* 26, 101-112.

Musto, D. (1997). "Historical perspectives." In *Substance Abuse: A Comprehensive Textbook,* Third Edition (J. Lowinson, P. Ruiz, R. Millman, and J. Langrod, eds.). Baltimore: Williams and Wilkins.

Musto, D. (1998). Interview. *Hooked: Illegal Drugs and How They Got That Way,* Volume 1, *Marijuana and Methamphetamine/Opium, Morphine and Heroin.* The History Channel. A&E Television Networks, 2000.

Nadelmann, E. (1989). Drug prohibition in the United States: Costs, consequences and alternatives. *Science,* 245(1 September), 939-947.

Nadelmann, E. (1992). Drug prohibition in the United States: Costs, consequences and alternatives. In *Drugs, Crime, and Social Policy* (Thomas Mieczkowski, ed.). Boston: Allyn and Bacon, pp. 299-322.

Narcotics Enforcement & Prevention Digest (2002a). 8(6), pp. 1-2.

Narcotics Enforcement & Prevention Digest (2002b). 8(14), August 30, pp. 1-2.

Nation, M., Crusto, C., Wandersman, A., Kumpfer, K., Seybolt, D., Morrissey-Kane, E., and Davino, K. (2003). What works in prevention. *American Psychologist,* 58(6-7), 449-456.

National Drug Intelligence Center (2001). Illinois drug threat assessment. Available online at: http://www.usdoj.gov/ndic/pubs/652/heroin.htm.

ONDCP (1994). "Measuring heroin availability in three cities." Executive Office of the ONDCP President, November.

ONDCP (2001a). Annual Report—"National Drug Control Strategy: Performance Measures of Effectiveness." PREX 26.1/2: 2001/perfor

ONDCP (2001b). "What America's Users Spend on Illegal Drugs." Executive Office of the President, December, p. 19.

Palfai, T., and Jankiewicz, H. (1997). *Drugs and Human Behavior,* Second Edition. Madison, WI: Brown and Benchmark, pp. 365-381.

Perrine, D. (1996). *The Chemistry of Mind-Altering Drugs.* Washington, DC: American Chemical Society, p. 47.

President's Advisory Commission on Narcotic and Drug Abuse (1963). *Final Report.* Wasington, DC: Government Printing Office.

Progression to Established Smoking: Results of a Longitudinal Youth Study (2000). *American Journal of Public Health,* 90(3), 380-386.

Rempel, R. and DeStefano, C. (2001). Predictors of engagement in court-mandated treatment: Findings at the Brooklyn Treatment Court, 1996-2000. In *Drug Courts in Operation: Current Research* (J. Hennessy and N. Pallone, eds.). Binghamton, NY: The Haworth Press, pp. 87-124.

Rosenbaum, D., and Hanson, G. (1998). Assessing the effects of school-based drug education: A six- year, multi-level analysis of Project DARE. *Journal of Research in Crime and Delinquency,* 35(4), 381-412.

Sanders, B., Wilkinson, C., and Allsop, S. (1991). "Motivational intervention with heroin users attending a methadone clinic." In *Motivational Interviewing: Preparing People to Change Addictive Behavior* (W. Miller and S. Rollnick, eds.). New York: Guilford Press.

Scalia, J. (2001). *Federal Drug Offenders, 1999, with Trends, 1984-99.* Washington, DC: Department of Justice, Bureau of Justice Statistics.

Schmoke, K. (1988). "Decriminalizing drugs: It just might work and nothing else does." In *Drugs and Drug Policy in America: A Documentary History* (S. Belenko, ed.), 2000. Westport, CT: Greenwood Press.

Shepard, E. (2001). *The Economic Costs of DARE.* Research Paper Number 22, Institute of Industrial Relations, LeMoyne College.

Shope, J., Copeland, L., and Marcoux, B. (1996). Effectiveness of a school-based substance abuse prevention program. *Journal of Drug Education,* 26(4), 323-337.

Siegel, M., and Biener, L. (2000). The impact of an antismoking media campaign on progression to established smoking: Reults of a longitudinal youth study. *American Journal of Public Health,* 90(3), 380-386.

Skager, R. (2001). On reinventing drug education, especially for adolescents. *The Reconsider Quarterly,* 1(4), pp. 14-18.

Stephens, Richard. (1992). Psychoactive drug use in the United States: A critical overview. In *Drugs, Crime, and Social Policy* (Thomas Mieczkowski, ed.). Boston: Allyn and Bacon, pp. 1-31.

Substance Abuse and Mental Health Services Administration. (2003). *Overview of Findings from the 2002 National Survey on Drug Use and Health (Office of Applied Studies, NHSDA Series H-21, DHHS Publication No. SMA 03–3774).* Rockville, MD. Author.

Swisher, J. (1979). Prevention Issues. In *Handbook on Drug Abuse* (DuPont et al., eds.). Washington, DC: National Institute of Drug Abuse.

Thornton, Mark (1991). Alcohol prohibition was a failure. *Cato Policy Analysis No. 157.* Washington, DC: The Cato Institute.

Tonrey, Michael (Ed.) (1992). "Mandatory Penalties." In *Crime and Justice: A Review of Research,* Chicago: University of Chicago Press Journals, pp. 243-244.

Torruella, J. (1996). *One Judge's Attempt at a Rational Discussion of the So-Called "War on Drugs."* Lecture at Colby College, Waterville, ME. Available at <http://www.vcl.org/Judges/Torruella_J.htm>.

United Nations (2000). *World Drug Report 2000.* United Nations Office for Drug Control and Crime Prevention. Oxford U. Press.

U.S. Congress (1924). *Hearings Before the Committee on Ways and Means of the House of Representatives.* 68th Cong., 1st sess. on HR 7079.

U.S. Congress, House of Rep. (1999). *The Decriminalization of Illegal Drugs: Hearing Before the Subcommittee on Criminal Justice, Drug Policy and Human Resources of the Committee on Government Reform.* 107th Cong., 1st sess., July 13.

U.S. Congress, House of Rep. (2001). *Drug Trade and the Terror Network: Hearing Before the Subcommittee on Criminal Justice, Drug Policy and Human Resources of the Committee on Government Reform.* 107th Cong., 1st sess., October 3.

U.S. Congress, Senate (1906). *Senate Docuyment 265.* 59th Cong., 1st sess., Serial Set Volume 4914, pp. 1-283. Washington, DC: Government Printing Office.

U.S. Congress, Senate (2001). *Treatment, Education and Prevention: Adding to the Arsenal in the War on Drugs.* Hearing Before the Committee on the Judiciary, March 14, 2001, p. 12.

U.S. Congress, Senate (2002). *Narco-Terror: The Worldwide Connection Between Drugs and Terrorism. Hearing Before the Subcommittee on Technology, Terrorism, and Government Information of the Committee on the Judiciary.* 107th Cong., 2nd sess., March 13.

U.S. Congressional Record (1913). Vol. 50(3), 2191-2211.

U.S. Senate Reports (1914). Vol. 1, of the 63rd Congress, 2nd sess. on Senate Bill 6552, report #258, February 18, pp. 3-4.

Vanyur, J., and Strada, F. (2002). Moving toward a comprehensive drug control strategy in prisons. *Corrections Today,* 64(5), 60-62; 126.

Walker, Samuel (1985). *Sense and Nonsense About Crime: A Policy Guide.* Monterey, CA: Brooks/Cole.

Walmsley, R. (2003). *World Prison Population List,* Fourth Edition. London, England: Home Office Research, Development and Statistics Directorate, p. 1.

Walsh, G. (1981). *Opium and Narcotic Laws.* Washington, DC: Government Printing Office.

Ybarra, I. (2004) *"Where Things Go Well for Me, There Is My Country": Repatriation in San Antonio During the Great Depression.* Available at http://colfa.utsa.edu:16080/users/jreynolds/Ybarra/part3.htm.

Index

Page numbers followed by the letter "f" indicate figures; those followed by the letter "t" indicate tables.